Taking one's own Life

Irene Sagel-Grande

Taking one's own Life

Euthanasia and Suicide in Dutch Law with a short excursus
to German Law

PETER LANG

Bibliografische Information der Deutschen Nationalbibliothek
Die Deutsche Nationalbibliothek verzeichnet diese Publikation
in der Deutschen Nationalbibliografie; detaillierte bibliografische
Daten sind im Internet über http://dnb.d-nb.de abrufbar.

ISBN 978-3-631-86865-2 (Print)
E-ISBN 978-3-631-87001-3 (E-PDF)
E-ISBN 978-3-631-87002-0 (EPUB)
DOI 10.3726/b19301

© Peter Lang GmbH
Internationaler Verlag der Wissenschaften
Berlin 2022
Alle Rechte vorbehalten.

Peter Lang – Berlin · Bern · Bruxelles · New York ·
Oxford · Warszawa · Wien

Diese Publikation wurde begutachtet.

www.peterlang.com

Table of Contents

Introduction 11

Part 1 The development of Euthanasia and Law from the
beginning until 2017 13

1. The development of the legal regulation, its practice, and a
new draft bill 13

   1.1. The development until the introduction of the Dutch
Law on Euthanasia 2001 13

   1.2. Terminology 13

   1.3. Special Dutch Criminal Law aspects, and their
influence on the development of the application of
law in the Netherlands in general, and especially in
connection with euthanasia 14

   1.4. The development in practice until 2005 15

      1.4.1. Important judgments 1952 until 1986 16

         1.4.1.1. The Postma Case 16

         1.4.1.2. The Wertheim Case 17

         1.4.1.3. The Schoonheim Case 18

      1.4.2. Criminal policy discussions on euthanasia
between 1984 and 1992 19

         1.4.2.1. The bill Wessel - Tuinstra 19

         1.4.2.2. The Royal Netherlands Medical Society
(KNMG) 19

         1.4.2.3. The State Commission Remmelink and
the research by Van der Maas c. s. 19

      1.4.3. Important judgments between 1992 and 2002 20

         1.4.3.1. The Chabot Case 20

         1.4.3.2. The Brongersma Case 21

2. Special provisions developed for the practice of euthanasia
and assisted suicide 22

   2.1. The institution of SCEN doctors 22

2.2. The obligation to report 23

2.3. The Regional Review Committees for termination of
life on request and assisted suicide 24

2.4. Empirical research and the evaluation of the reporting
procedure between 1990 and 1995 24

3. The Dutch Law on Euthanasia in full "Termination of Life
on Request and Assisted Suicide (Review Procedures) Act
2001" 25

3.1. Introduction 25

3.2. The content of the Dutch Law on Euthanasia 27

3.2.1. Chapters I and II 27

3.2.2. Chapter III 27

3.2.3. Chapter IV 28

3.2.3.1. Main amendments in the Criminal Code . 28

3.2.3.2. Main amendments in the Burial and
Cremation Act 29

3.3. The Review Procedures step by step 30

3.4. Euthanasia and Dementia 31

3.5. Evaluations of the Law on Euthanasia 32

3.5.1. Introduction 32

3.5.2. General findings 2011 33

3.5.3. Some important results of the evaluations 2011
and 2017 33

3.6. Results of the introduction of the Law on Euthanasia 35

3.7. The latest Ministerial Order about prosecution
decisions concerning active termination of life on
request of the Department of Prosecution of the 17th
of May 2017 36

4. The State of Affairs in 2017 37

4.1. Introduction 37

4.2. The discussion on "The Right to Commit Suicide" in
recent years 38

4.3. A new draft-bill 39

4.4. The Dutch Society for Psychiatry 40

5. Final remarks 2017 40

Part 2 The development from 2017 until the end of 2021 43

  1. Introduction 43

  2. The coalition agreement 2017–2021 44

  3. Continuation and final judgment of the Heringa Case 45

  4. The "Perspective Research" 46

    4.1. Introduction 46

    4.2. The quantitative research 47

      4.2.1. The 21,294 interviewees aged 55 years and older 48

      4.2.2. The interviewed medical practitioners 50

    4.3. The qualitative research 51

      4.3.1. Introduction 51

      4.3.2. Experiences in connection with the wish to die 51

      4.3.3. The development of the death-wish in time 51

  5. The judgement of the Supreme Court of the Netherlands of
    April 21st, 2020 53

    5.1. Introduction and the facts of the case 53

    5.2. The most important considerations of the Supreme
      Court and their grounds in the criminal case 55

    5.3. The judgement of the Supreme Court in the respective
      disciplinary case 56

  6. The Royal Dutch Medical Association (KNMG) and the
    judgment of the Supreme Court of April 21st, 2020 57

  7. The introduction of the "Completed Life" draft-bill in
    parliament 59

  8. Euthanasia and palliative sedation 60

  9. Euthanasia and demented people 63

    9.1. Critical comments of the Health and Youth Inspection
      and the Medical Disciplinary Board 63

    9.2. The proposal to make euthanasia for demented elderly
      people possible already in an earlier state 65

    9.3. The chapter on demented people in the KNMG and
      KNMP (the Royal Dutch association for the promotion
      of Pharmacy) guideline "Implementation of Euthanasia
      and Assisted Suicide" 2021 67

10. Free access to lethal means? 68

11. Euthanasia and children beyond human aid, aged 1–12 years   74

12. Summary of the recent developments in the Netherlands   77

13. Excursus: The Corona Pandemic   77

**Part 3 Open questions and a view of the prospects of the
future**   83

    1. Facts and figures, important to find right answers   83

       1.1. Excursus: Suicide and euthanasia in history, the
lasting roots   83

       1.2. Present knowledge about human life and death in
natural science and psychology in a nutshell   87

       1.3. Causes of suicide and euthanasia   89

       1.4. Suicide, euthanasia, and age   91

       1.5. Dutch numbers of suicide in relation to some other
countries   92

       1.6. Suicide by gender   92

       1.7. Methods of taking one's own life   92

    2. Suicide, and euthanasia, right, and law   94

       2.1. The Dutch Constitution   94

       2.2. Human diversity, human dignity, and the need of self-
determination   97

       2.3. The German Constitution, human dignity, and an
unwritten right on self-determination   98

          2.3.1. The German Constitution   98

          2.3.2. The judgment of the German Federal
Constitutional Court on § 217 German
Criminal Law   100

          2.3.3. Two German draft-bills on suicide and suicide
assistance   101

       2.4. Summing-up   104

    3. Taking one's own Life, Dementia, and Human Dignity   105

    4. Outlook   107

4.1. Dutch public opinion and the Cooperation Last Will 107

4.2. Forward-looking in Jurisprudence 109

4.3. Waiting for the legislator 110

Part 4 Appendix 115

Bibliography 133

Some other publications of the same author (until 2021) 137

Introduction

The word "euthanasia" has its roots in a combination of the old Greek **"eu"** (good), and **"thanatos"** (death). "Suicide" has Latin roots and is a combination of **"sui"** (oneself) and **"caedere"** (hit, kill).

Some observations about euthanasia in ancient times are an adequate starting point as this manuscript was primarily written for a summer course in Thessaloniki and those ancient ideas about euthanasia are still of interest for our present discussions.

In those old days, the "good" death in Greece primarily had the meaning of dying nobly and manlike, the proper sense being passing away on the battlefield[1] and not, or at least much less, to escape from unbearable pain and sufferings.

Euthanasia was accepted as a possibility to take the honorable way and to save one's face, as something that was recognized as brave and heroic. It was also a manner for crowning one's life and therefore not the same for all people. Emperors, heroes, and philosophers were choosing their own model of euthanatein which means to die honorably.[2]

Some examples are as follows: About **Meander** it was reported that he used the word euthanatos for a death without a long time of illness, thus a relatively quick death. For **Socrates** (469–399 B.C.) the right preparation for death after a responsible life belonged to euthanasia,[3] while for **Seneca** one had to pass away when signs of loosing one's dignity appear. By choosing euthanasia you prove yourself.[4]

In the Roman period euthanatein was primarily a passing away mildly and without pain. In Latin euthanasia was **"mors voluntaria"**, thus stressing the will of the actor. About the famous Emperor **Augustus** was reported that every time he heard that somebody died without pain, he wished a similar death for himself and his family.[5]

---

1 A. van Hooff, Euthanasie en zelfdoding in de klassieke oudheid, LEIF, interview on internet, 6-7-2010.
2 A. van Hooff, Euthanasie in de oudheid, "Ik rot weg in genot", Historisch Nieuwsblad 1/2003.
3 De.wikipedia.org/wiki-geschichte der Euthanasie: Meander & Sokrates & Augustus.
4 A. van Hooff, see above.
5 Suetonius, The Life of Augustus. Oxford 2014.

The old Greeks already had different answers concerning the question whether men have the right to commit euthanasia or not.

According to the oath of **Hippocrates** (460–370 B.C.), the Greek physician who established medicine as a profession and is seen as the Father of Modern Medicine, nobody may hand any death-causing medicine to a person even not if he or she asks for it, and **Plato** (427–347 B.C.) stated that men are God's soldiers who have to stay on their duty until "God" calls them, but also meant that ill people who miss vital energy should no longer be treated. **Aristotle** (384–322 B.C.) based the obligation to live on a duty toward community, argued, however, that it is ethically sound to practice euthanasia in the interest of the state, for example, one should not invest in the bringing up of invalids. For **Pythagoras,** denying the duty to live was a rebellion against the gods. In classical Greek tragedies, however, those who committed suicide were often characterized as heroes.

In ancient times, medical doctors just had to help their patients without asking questions as the prevailing opinion was that the physician's acting was just a continuation of the will of the patient. As medical doctors often were slaves, there were hardly any problems with this view. The situation nowadays is totally different and makes it impossible to let a doctor fulfill your own will. According to Dutch classics scholar and cultural historian A. van Hooff,[6] classical antiquity can teach us to overcome our fear and shame of death, and at the same time, the antique model of dying well offers us the concept of the fundamental right of self-determination we nowadays are missing.

February 2022

---

6 A. van Hooff, see above.

Part 1 The development of Euthanasia and Law from the beginning until 2017

1. The development of the legal regulation, its practice, and a new draft bill

1.1. The development until the introduction of the Dutch Law on Euthanasia 2001

Before we can focus on the Dutch legal regulations on euthanasia, we have to say something about (1) the terminology, (2) about special Dutch Penal Law provisions that offer possibilities to handle problems that occur in society in the legal sphere at least partly without necessarily amending or changing the law and (3) about the developments in legal practice and society that finally led to the introduction of the legal regulation presently in force.

1.2. Terminology

The Dutch Law on Euthanasia of the 12th of April 2001, in full: Termination of Life on Request and Assisted Suicide (Review Procedure) Act[7] came into force on the 1st of April 2002. It was worldwide the first law that regulates euthanasia. Similar laws came into force shortly after in Belgium and in Luxemburg.

The definition for euthanasia in the Dutch Law on Euthanasia[8] reads:

Euthanasia is the intentional termination of the life of another person on this person's request.
This definition is also used by the Belgian legislator. It focusses only on the so-called active euthanasia.

No euthanasia according to the Dutch Law on Euthanasia are:

- Abandoning senseless treatment
- Abandoning treatment on request of the patient

---

7   Bulletin of Acts, Orders and Decrees of the Kingdom of the Netherlands (Staatsblad) 2001, p. 194.
8   The same definition was already used by the State Commission Euthanasia 1983: Report of the Royal Commission Euthanasia, Staatsuitgeverij, ISBN90-12-05113.

- Palliative sedation: A patient suffering from heavy pain is rendered unconscious with strong pain reducing drugs and eventually dies from natural causes.

Assisted suicide is defined in the Dutch Law on Euthanasia as intentionally assisting in a suicide of another person or procuring for that other person the means to commit suicide.

As far as the persons involved are fully accountable patients and medical doctors, there is no real difference between euthanasia and assisted suicide. In both cases the medical doctor provides the lethal means in an adequate dose and supervises that these means are applied correctly. Decisive for the definition of what happened before the death of a patient is who performed the last necessary doings. If the patient is suffering from dementia and the lethal means are given based on a declaration of intention written in the past, the event must be categorized as euthanasia.

There are not always the same definitions used for one and the same subject by the writers and not all terms are in use by all writers. In this contribution the definition of the Dutch legislator is adopted.

1.3. Special Dutch Criminal Law aspects, and their influence on the development of the application of law in the Netherlands in general, and especially in connection with euthanasia

In Dutch criminal law the principle of discretionary powers plays an important role. We find it in the articles 167 sub 2 and art. 242 sub 2 Code of Criminal Procedure. It is in force not only for minor offences but generally for all delicts and offers the public prosecutors the possibility to drop prosecution for the sake of expediency by reasons deriving from common good and public interest. This Dutch principle of expediency is a consequence of the idea that criminal law mainly is in aid of the common good and that the available criminal law means must be used as efficiently as possible to realize the main criminal law aims that are prevention and retaliation.

The Dutch principle of expediency is a good and successful means for the Department of Public Prosecution to apply the law in practice continuously while criminal policy changes and important developments in society take place.

Besides for the public prosecutor, Dutch criminal law also offers means for the judges to take a lenient view and corresponding decisions on cases as the Dutch law knows in its sanction system low general minima, thus no regularly special minima for the different offences. The fine has nota bene a general minimum of € 3[9] and the prison sentence a general minimum of one day![10]

The most common crime against life, manslaughter, art. 287 Dutch Criminal Code, can for example be punished with a prison sentence between the general minimum of 1 day and the special maximum of 15 years or a fine between the general minimum of € 3 and the special maximum of € 87,000[11]. The highest fine (6th category) is since the 1st of January 2020: € 870,000.

By sentencing a judge who is convinced that somebody committed even manslaughter thus has a very wide discretionary power for special cases although this power has several limits deriving for example from practice and tradition of jurisdiction and the influence of the demands for punishment by the public prosecutors. Nevertheless, the judges have great decision-making powers in sentencing and can use this power, to take into consideration not only the special circumstances of the offence and the peculiarities of the offender but also new social developments and the actual public opinion concerning the criminal act in question and the kind of sentencing awaited and accepted in society.

Euthanasia and assisted suicide are still generally punishable in the Netherlands.

Euthanasia can be punished with a prison sentence from the general minimum of one day up to the special maximum of 12 years, respectively, a fine from € 3 to € 87,000.

In cases of **assisted suicide,** the judge principally has the possibility to fix the sentence out of a range of punishments for what concerns a prison sentence of the general minimum of 1 day and the special maximum for assisted suicide of 3 years, in the case of a fine between the general minimum of 3 €, and the special maximum for assisted suicide of € 21,750.[12]

1.4. The development in practice until 2005

Before the present legal regulation was introduced in the Netherlands, the subjects euthanasia and assisted suicide were heavily discussed again and again during decennia by various organizations and instances, in the media and in state commissions, bills were worked out that did not pass parliament and empirical research took place to get more knowledge about what happens in practice and what the public opinion was like.

---

9   Art. 23 sub 2 Dutch Criminal Code (October 2020).
10 Art. 10 sub 2 Dutch Criminal Code (October 2020).
11 Art. 23 sub 4 Dutch Criminal Code.
12 Art. 23 sub 4 per 01-01-2020.

During this long period of often very emotional discussions in which the different opinions clashed in fierce struggle the public interest in euthanasia was growing. Sentences in cases of physicians who did euthanasia were taken up by the media and this provoked an increasing public interest in the punishment of these practitioners. Furthermore, during this period certain methods of handling euthanasia developed at the courts based on and in agreement with the described special Dutch criminal law principles that offer the possibility to take new developments in society into account, without the need of legislation.

1.4.1. Important judgments 1952 until 1986

Already in **1952**, a medical doctor who gave his heavily suffering brother tablets and a mortal injection was convicted to a relatively mild sanction, namely a suspended prison sentence of one year.[13]

1.4.1.1. The Postma Case

In **1974**, the so-called Leeuwarden case created a great stir.[14] A medical doctor gave her 78 years old, extremely suffering mother who had repeatedly asked to be delivered from her pain, on the 19th of October 1971 a mortal injection morphine in a home for elderly people. In its conclusion the court considered that an act that shortens a life can be justified under certain circumstances, but it did not accept the plead of the medical doctor for circumstances beyond her control, as the court observed that the method, which she used was wrong. The judgment of the district court Leeuwarden was a week suspended prison sentence with a probation period of one year! It was the first important judgment on euthanasia in the Netherlands, not only for its sensationally low punishment in a case of homicide but perhaps even more for the fact that it summarized the conditions for euthanasia for the first time in the Netherlands as there are:

Terminal stage of an incurable illness,
subjective unbearable bodily or psychical suffering,
no chance of getting better,
a written request of the patient, and
the implementation by a medical doctor.

---

13   Nederlandse Jurisprudentie 1952, p. 275.
14   Leeuwarden is a Dutch city. Nederlandse Jurisprudentie 1973, p. 183.

In later jurisdiction the existence of these conditions became decisive for the answer to the question whether a case of euthanasia or assisted suicide existed or not.

The Postma case was the immediate cause to establish the Dutch Society for Voluntary Euthanasia in 1973 in Vinkega, Friesland, since 2006 named the Dutch Society for a Voluntary End of Life (NVVE). The society seeks to get the right to choose a voluntary end of life and the necessary help that is needed hereby recognized as a Human Right. In 2015, when the Netherlands had about 16.9 million inhabitants, the NVVE had about 163,000 members. This number is steadily growing. At the NVVE office in Amsterdam 30 staff members were working at the end of 2019.[15]

1.4.1.2. The Wertheim Case

In 1981, the district court in Rotterdam had to decide the Wertheim Case in which a woman, not being a medical doctor, assisted another woman in committing suicide.[16] On her request the latter who was an alcoholic and was convinced that she had cancer and her life had been a disaster since her youth, got the deadly medicine from her friend.

The court considered in this case

- that nowadays, according to many people and differing from what one generally thought at the time the Criminal Code came into force in 1881, suicide in exceptional cases is no longer per se unacceptable. Moreover, the court held that it is of great importance for those directly involved, for acquaintances as well as for people in the direct surrounding, that suicide does not happen under cruel circumstances and is something one generally is not able to do alone.

Furthermore, the Rotterdam district court refers to the criteria summarized by the district court Leeuwarden in the **Postma Case of 1973** (see above) and then adds further conditions of carefulness: It provides namely that the decision to help in cases of euthanasia and assisted suicide may not be taken by one person

---

15 Nederlandse Vereniging voor een Vrijwillig Levenseinde (NVVE), Financieel Jaarverslag 2019.

16 Nederlandse Jurisprudentie 1982, p. 63.

alone and that always a medical doctor must be involved who must prescribe the drug to be used.

In the Wertheim case the district court concluded that most of the necessary conditions for an assisted suicide were missing. Accordingly, it decided that if the circumstances beyond one's control were not present assisted suicide (art. 294 Criminal Code) can be held as proven. The district court sentenced the offender to a conditional prison sentence of 6 months with a probation period of one year.

1.4.1.3. The Schoonheim Case

Shortly later, **between 1983 and 1986,** the Schoonheim Case brought a further development in the acceptance of euthanasia by the courts. The district court in Alkmaar discharged a medical doctor from prosecution who gave an old woman on her earnest and explicit request a deadly injection. The district court's argumentation was that the right to self-determination in connection with the end of one's own life is meanwhile accepted by many people in society. To realize this right in an acceptable manner, one needs the help of someone else and that is the reason why, in cases of the voluntarily ending one's life, this assistance, although it is generally criminalized, is not punishable. The help of a third person is conflicting with the text of the law but not with its aim. However, the absence of material unlawfulness in cases of this kind can only be accepted if there was an earnest, deliberate, and conscious request of the patient based on severe long-lasting suffering and if everything happened with great carefulness.

The considerations of the district court in Alkmaar remind us of the ideas in ancient times when the will of the person who asks for euthanasia was recognized as the only will, responsible for all that happens in connection with this person's death.

It was for the first time in the Schoonheim Case that a Dutch district court found a case of euthanasia (art. 293 Criminal Code) proved, but not punishable.

This judgment was reversed by the court of appeal in Amsterdam, which declared absence of material unlawfulness as well as a state of emergency, not present, and accordingly found the medical doctor guilty but nevertheless did not impose a sanction.

The Supreme Court referred the case to the court of appeal in The Hague. At this occasion, the Supreme Court for the first time stated something in relation to euthanasia, asserting that euthanasia principally can be permitted under certain conditions in cases of emergency.

In **1986,** the court of appeal in The Hague concluded that in the Schoonheim Case a situation of emergency was given and acquitted the medical doctor from prosecution.

1.4.2. Criminal policy discussions on euthanasia between 1984 and 1992

1.4.2.1. The bill Wessel - Tuinstra

Before the next spectacular judgment on euthanasia became known in 1993 a bill was presented by Mrs. Wessel -Tuinstra, a member of parliament for the social-liberal party **in 1984.** This bill proposed to decriminalize euthanasia[17] for those who offer help and act carefully in totally hopeless emergency cases. In parliament this bill got no majority in 1993 mainly because it was thought to be not in accordance with the public opinion.

1.4.2.2. The Royal Netherlands Medical Society (KNMG[18])

In **1984,** the Royal Netherlands Dutch Medical Society published for the first time the conditions, medical doctors according to the opinion of their organization must meet in cases of euthanasia and assisted suicide. Since then, also the courts have incorporated these conditions in their jurisdiction: Deliberate request, serious considerations, continuing wish to terminate the own life, serious unbearable illness, and the consultation of a colleague.

1.4.2.3. The State Commission Remmelink and the research by Van der Maas c. s.[19]

In **1987,** a new bill[20] was prepared and **in 1990** the State Commission Remmelink was installed. This commission initiated for the first time, empirical research on euthanasia, assisted suicide and end of life without request. In the first place one wanted to know how often the respective acts took place.

The result of this research was that there were less cases than generally supposed. About 1.8% of all deaths were cases of euthanasia and yearly about 400 cases of assisted suicide became known in the Netherlands (by then about 15 million inhabitants). Furthermore, it was found that in the Netherlands yearly

---

17 Tweede Kamer (Second Chamber /Lower House)1984 no. 18331.
18 Koninklijke Nederlandse Maatschappij tot Bevordering der Geneeskunst.
19 Nederlands Tijdschrift voor Geneeskunde 1991, p. 2073.
20 Tweede Kamer 1987,1988 no. 20383.

about 9,000 persons intended to end their life. Main reasons were the fear to lose one's human dignity (57%) and unbearable pain (46%).

This information is surely of interest however one should not take it as hard facts as there are several difficulties in collecting these data, differences in terminology, insecurities in the interpretation of the facts by the respondents, and conscious and unconscious inaccuracies in reporting. They all can cause a significant grey area.

The report of the Commission Remmelink set forth that euthanasia mostly takes place at the patient's home with the help of the family doctor and that the physicians principally all act very carefully.

For the Dutch Minister of Justice, the results of the work of the Commission Remmelink were the reason to declare that an amendment of the Criminal Code was not necessary as the practice developed by the public prosecutors and the courts already guarantee a satisfying solution of the problem.[21]

1.4.3. Important judgments between 1992 and 2002

1.4.3.1. The Chabot Case

In 1991, a woman took the lethal medicine she got from her psychiatrist. The woman was not ill, had no psychiatric disorder but was earnestly suffering since many years from grief and sorrow combined with depressions caused by a bad marriage followed by a divorce and the death of her two sons. After she attempted to commit suicide, she got acquainted with the psychiatrist Chabot.

In court decisions, by then, there was never differentiation before between bodily and psychic suffering and furthermore until the Case Chabot never, there was a case to be decided on by a judge in which no somatic or psychiatric disorder could be diagnosed.

The judges at the district court in Assen were focussing only on the questions whether the woman was unbearably suffering without a perspective to become better and whether her request was as well the result of serious as of free consideration. For the first time in Dutch jurisdiction, the suffering was extricated from the underlying illness. The judges thought the reasons for suffering were not relevant and concluded that in the case in question the psychiatrist assisted his patient to commit suicide according to art. 294 Criminal Code. As Chabot acted meticulously and well-considered, the judges were convinced that circumstances beyond one's control were present and acquitted him.

---

21 Tweede Kamer 1991/1992 no. 20383.

In **1993**, the court of appeal in Leeuwarden came to the same conclusions.
The Supreme Court[22] followed the opinions of the judges of both instances widely but stated that Chabot was in default concerning one point. He refrained from having his patient seen by a second psychiatrist and declared Chabot therefore guilty without imposing a sentence according to art. 9 a Dutch Criminal Code where, among other reasons the judge can decide that regarding the personality of the offender, it is not necessary to impose a sanction.

1.4.3.2. *The Brongersma Case*

In **April 1998,** Edward Brongersma, 87 years old, died after he had taken the medicine, his doctor gave him. Brongersma was a lawyer, writer, member of the Socialist Party (PvdA) and for this party member of the Dutch Senate. He was not ill, but his health was no longer strong and after the death of his best friends he was lonely, and his life had become unbearable for him according to his opinion.

In **October 2000**, the district court in Haarlem had to decide this case. The main question hereby was whether in the case of Brongersma one could really speak of unbearable hopeless suffering. The judges stated that there is no common opinion in medical ethics whether the definition of "unbearable" must be narrow or wide. The district court in Haarlem chose for a wide interpretation insofar and was furthermore convinced that Brongersma had no real chance for a better future. As doctor Sutorius acted meticulously, all generally necessary preconditions to accept Sutorius's appeal to circumstances beyond one's control existed and accordingly the district court in Haarlem found Sutorius not guilty.

The competent public prosecutor, however, doubted whether the suffering of Brongersma could be judged as being "unbearable" and "hopeless". According to his opinion Brongersma was weary of life or ready with life, both situations that as such do not belong to the medical domain of euthanasia.

The court of appeal in Amsterdam decided in 2001 that two experts should make a medical assessment about the kind of Brongersma's suffering. Half a year later both experts concluded that Brongersma's suffering was something that does not belong to the medical field. The court of appeal in Amsterdam found doctor Sutorius thus guilty but imposed no sentence. It pointed out that the discussion about assisted suicide in cases in which the unbearable and hopeless suffering is not the consequence of illness had only just started.

---

22 Hoge Raad (HR) (Dutch Supreme Court) 21-6-1994, Nederlandse Jurisprudentie (NJ) 1994, p. 646.

Sutorius's appeal in cassation resulted in a decision of the Supreme Court that follows the decision of the court of appeal in Amsterdam and declares Sutorius guilty[23] because "the recent developments of legislation on euthanasia"- the Law on Euthanasia that will be discussed here soon had by then entered into force -, show that the legislator obviously is not willing to let cases of being "ready with life" belong to those of euthanasia.

2. Special provisions developed for the practice of euthanasia and assisted suicide

The most important of these provisions are (1) the SCEN doctors, (2) the obligation to report, (3) the installment of committees to examine whether the involved medical doctors exercised due care and (4) regular empirical research.

2.1. The institution of SCEN doctors

Many physicians are only very exceptionally getting in touch with a request to terminate the life of one of their patients and therefore they are not experienced with its practice. To help them, the Royal Dutch Medical Association introduced the specialism of so called SCEN physicians. SCEN means Support and Consultation in cases of Euthanasia in the Netherlands. Via SCEN, medical doctors who were asked to terminate the life of one of their patients or to assist them committing suicide have the possibility to get in contact with a colleague who can give them an expert opinion concerning the question whether in the concrete case due care is exercised. Per family doctor district a physician can contact by phone such a specially trained colleague. SCEN doctors cannot be contacted by the family doctor with just the request to take over the termination of life, but with all relevant questions concerning the procedure, medical-technical questions, ethical questions, and communication problems belonging to the field. The institution of the SCEN doctors meanwhile already exists since about 20 years and is surely of great importance for relatively unexperienced family doctors who want to help their patients and to act with due care. SCEN also supports the readiness of medical doctors to accept the requests of their patients.

---

23 24-12-2002, Nederlandse Jurisprudentie (NJ) 2003, p. 167.

2.2. The obligation to report

All actions of medical doctors that cause the end of human life must be reported to the medical officer of health, who is obliged to inform the public prosecutor about the reports he received. Before the Law on Euthanasia was in force, the public prosecutor could wave the cases in which the medical doctor acted on the patient's request and the deed could be justified in the framework of the principle of expediency. At present the Law on Euthanasia with its criminal defence regulates these cases.

If there is no explicit request the public prosecutor will generally start prosecuting.

The definite decision in these cases is taken by the Advocates General who meet regularly to discuss all criminal policy problems and to prepare orders and guidelines addressed to the subordinate public prosecutors, mainly, to guarantee uniformity in prosecution.

The system of registration of principally all cases of euthanasia already got a legal basis by the Law of the 2nd of December 1993 that amended the Burial and Cremation Act[24]. It provides that in cases the pathologist who performs the autopsy is not willing to provide a certification of death, the pathologist must report to the public prosecutor. Form and content of this report must be regulated by Order in Council of State, a subordinate regulation. In 1993, the first respective order came into force. It regulates the subject in detail and prescribes the use of a model form.[25]

In 1998, a revised text about the registration procedure in cases of ending a life on explicit request by a medical doctor came into force.[26] Since then, one differentiates between euthanasia and assisted suicide on explicit request and the cases without such a request. The respective ordonnance does not cover the cases of people who are not able to form their will. Therefore, in these cases, except for malformed newly born children or babies with extremely bad health, the public prosecutor must examine every case thoroughly. The legislator relied so far on the practice in which the same differentiation was already developed, and prosecution was regularly found to be not necessary in cases in which the

---

24 Bulletin of Acts, Orders and Decrees (Staatsblad) 1993, p. 643.
25 Bulletin of Acts, Orders and Decrees (Staatsblad) 1993, p. 688.
26 Statutory Instrument of 19-11-1997, p. 550 about Art. 10 Interment Law mentioned forms for cases of unnatural death that do not belong to the cases without explicit request.

patient after careful deliberation earnestly and repeatedly had declared his wish to end his life.

2.3. The Regional Review Committees for termination of life on request and assisted suicide

In connection with the reform of the reporting procedures there were five regional committees introduced (Arnhem, Den Bosch, Groningen, Haarlem, and Rijswijk) that got the task to examine termination of life on request (euthanasia) and assisted suicide. As members physicians, lawyers, and experts in the field of ethics in medical matters are elected. The reason for the introduction of these committees was primarily to place the decisions of the public prosecutors on a broader basis. The five committees do not restrict the power of the public prosecutor, the prosecutors however, should be open for the arguments of the committees.

The committees started their work on the 1st of November 1998. They have three members, one of each profession, and a secretary each. Their task is to examine, based on valid criteria, that were developed by court practice, whether the medical doctors acted in the individual cases according to their duty of care. The committees send their reports to the Advocates General, to the Local Health Authorities, and to the respective physician. On a medical doctor's request, the committee also has the task to explain the committee's decision to inform the medical doctor about the criteria in use by the committee.

Furthermore, it belongs to the tasks of the committees to give their opinion concerning euthanasia and assisted suicide in individual cases to medical doctors before they decide to comply or not with the requests in the concrete cases.

When a committee is convinced that the medical doctor acted thoroughly, the public prosecutor will regularly discontinue prosecution.

Details concerning prosecution in cases of ending life by request were put down for the first time in an Order in 1998 that came into force together with the start of the work of the five committees on the 1st of November 1998.

2.4. Empirical research and the evaluation of the reporting procedure between 1990 and 1995 [27]

A rather remarkable result of the first empirical research on euthanasia was that in cases of euthanasia and assisted suicide the shortening of life was generally relatively

---

27 P. J. van der Maas, Nederlands Tijdschrift voor Geneeskunde 1997, p. 98, I. Sagel-Grande, Rechtliche Regelung der Euthanasie in den Niederlanden, Zeitschrift für die gesamte Strafrechtswissenschaft 111 (1999), p. 742.

little: in 17% of cases less than 24 hours, in 42% one day to one week, in 32% one week to 4 weeks, and in 9% more than one month.

Another important result of this research was that not all cases were reported. In 1995 these were not more than 41%.

The results of the evaluation of the reporting procedures[28] became the basis for the changes mentioned already above[29], namely the obligation to report and the introduction of the review committees.

3. The Dutch Law on Euthanasia in full "Termination of Life on Request and Assisted Suicide (Review Procedures) Act 2001"

3.1. Introduction

The aim of the Dutch Law on Euthanasia was primarily to codify what was developed by and by during several decennia until about the end of the 20th century. It is a codification based on the experience of medical and judicial professionals, of what practitioners who are daily confronted with the problems and conflicts of their patients, respectively of the medical doctors, family members, and friends of the patients, they must prosecute or sentence. It became a law in which professional knowledge, a long practical experience, the legal responsibilities of physicians, public prosecutors, and judges, and the ethical standards they are bound to, are combined to conform with standards of humanity. Dogmatic and theoretical considerations were not influential, but something that becomes obvious by its content, structure and use of language. All is focusing on practice, not at least the way the review procedures are emphasized.

That the Law on Euthanasia finally after so many years of very heavy and controversial discussions in politics and society could be realized is for an important part the result of the growing secularization that took place in the Netherlands in the second half of the 20th century. While in 1958 24% of the Dutch population was nonreligious this percentage was 64% in 2004. The Catholics declined in the same period from 42% to 17% and the protestants from 31% to 10% of the Dutch population.[30]

---

28 I. Sagel-Grande, The decriminalisation of Euthanasia in the Netherlands, Acta Criminologica, vol. 11, 1998, p. 104–112; s. Annex.

29 Kamerstukken (Parliamentary Documents) 1996/1997, nr. 23 877 sub 13.

30 J. Becker, J. de Hart, L. Arnts, Godsdienstige veranderingen in Nederland, Den Haag 2006, p. 38.

The Roman Catholic Church still considers all kinds of acting and refraining that intend to cause the death of a person to end pain and suffering as murder.[31] Using analgesics, however, is allowed even if they shorten life so far as the death is neither the aim nor the means.[32] The Protestants and the Jews are also principally opponents of euthanasia.

The Law on Euthanasia passed parliament with the votes of the left-wing Liberals (Democrats 66), the right-wing Liberals (Party for Freedom and Democracy), and the Socialist Party. A decisive role in the adoption of the law had Els Borst, physician and member of the left-wing Liberal "Democrats 66" who at that time was Minister of Public Health and as such responsible for the Law on Euthanasia. According to her opinion, the Law on Euthanasia as it finally was adopted presents a decent regulation. In an interview with NRC/Handelsblad two days after the law was adopted, being nota bene a Good Friday, she used the Word from the Cross, "It is done". This made many Christians furious, also many members of the Christian Parties in parliament. Later Els Borst apologized in parliament. This event can only be understood if one knows that still nowadays there are areas in the Netherlands, generally an enlightened rather modern country, where people are extremely orthodox and, for example have their children not vaccinated for religious reasons.

The life of Els Borst ended in a sort of classical tragedy. She was terribly cruelly murdered on the 14th of February 2014 in her house with 41 stabs of a knife, also into her eyes. In January 2015 traces of DNA of a 38-years old man, Bart van U., `were found on clothes of Els Borst. Shortly before, and 11 months after the murder of Els Borst, he had murdered one of his sisters with a knife with whom he lived together in a house in Rotterdam. According to the statement of Van U., he killed his sister for reasons of self-defence. He testified that his relation to this sister had been bad because she had a different opinion about abortion and euthanasia. In relation to the murder on Els Borst, Van U. made use of his right to remain silent. Only on the 4th of February 2016, almost 2 years after the murder of Els Borst, he was willing to make a statement and confessed that he was ordered by God to kill Els Borst for her responsibility for the Law on Euthanasia and the Law on Abortion. Van U. grew up in an Orthodox-Christian surrounding. He was schizophrenic and his family was very afraid of him.

---

31 Catechismus van de Katholieke Kerk 1992, § 2277.
32 Catechismus van de Katholieke Kerk 1992, § 2279.

Van U. was sentenced to 8 years imprisoment in appeal, immediately followed by hospital order for psychopaths with compulsory treatment without a fixed end because it was not predictable how long he would need treatment.

3.2. The content of the Dutch Law on Euthanasia

The Law on Euthanasia has four Chapters.

3.2.1. Chapters I and II

After the definitions of terms in Chapter I the requirements of due care referred to in art. 293 sub 2 Criminal Code are summarized in Chapter II, saying that the physician must be convinced that the request of the patient was voluntary and well considered and that the patient's suffering was lasting and unbearable (a. and b.).

Furthermore, the physician must have informed the patient about his or her situation and about his or her prospects and must have come together with the patient to the conviction, that there is no other reasonable solution for the situation the patient is in (c. and d.).

The physician must also have consulted at least one other independent physician who has seen the patient and has given his written opinion on the requirements of due care referred to above. Finally, the physician who terminated a life or assisted in a suicide must have exercised due care (e. and f.).

The law on Euthanasia is principally in force for persons aged 12 years and older as in the Netherlands children from 12 years on in accordance with the law can give informed consent. Therefore, they can also apply themselves for euthanasia and assisted suicide.

Precondition is, that they can judge their situation sensibly and that they are able to express their will. The parents or the guardian cannot make the request in the name of the juvenile. In cases of juveniles aged 12–15 years of age, the parents respectively the guardian, must agree. Juveniles between 16 and 17 years old can decide themselves, however, the parents or the guardian must be involved in the finding of the decision, Art. 2 sub 2-4 Law on Euthanasia.

3.2.2. Chapter III

Chapter III regulates the Regional Review Committees for the Termination of Life on Request and Assisted Suicide, their establishment and composition, appointment, dismissal, remuneration, duties and powers of their members, their working methods, that are laid down in detail by Ministerial Regulation of the

Ministers, secrecy and exemption and the duty to make annual reports on the activities of the past year for the Ministers, which must include at any rate

- the number of reported cases of termination of life on request and assisted suicide on which the committee has given an opinion,
- the nature of these cases and
- the opinions and considerations involved (art. 17 Law on Euthanasia).

3.2.3. Chapter IV

In **Chapter IV** we find the amendments to the Criminal Code, the Burial and Cremation Act and the General Administrative Law Act.

3.2.3.1. Main amendments in the Criminal Code

Already in the opening words to the Law on Euthanasia we find the main reasons for the coming into being of this law:

> "We Beatrix, by the grace of God Queen of The Netherlands, Princes of Orange-Nassau etc. etc. etc. ....

All who this will see or hear read, greetings! let know:

> We have taken in consideration that it is advisable to introduce into the Criminal Code a criminal defence for the physicians who regarding the by law established requirements of due care terminate a life on request or assist in a suicide and for that purpose provide for a reporting - and review procedure by law.

The criminal defence is formulated mainly in the Dutch Criminal Code in the articles 293 and 294:

Art. 293 Criminal Code as amended by the Law on Euthanasia reads as follows:

(1) A person who intentionally terminates the life of another person on the express and earnest request of that other person is liable to a term of imprisonment of not more than 12 years or a fine of the fifth category (€ 87,000[33]).

(2) The offence referred to sub (1) is not punishable if it was committed by a physician who met the requirements of due care meant in art. 2 Termination of Life on Request and Assisted Suicide (Review Procedures) Act 2001 and who informs the municipal autopsist of this fact in accordance with Art. 7 sub 2 of the Burial and Cremation Act.

Art. 294 Criminal Code as amended by the Law on Euthanasia reads as follows:

---

33 Since 1.1.2020, before: € 82,000.

(1) A person who intentionally incites another person to commit suicide is liable to a term of imprisonment of not more than three years or a fine of the fourth category (€ 21.750)[34] if the suicide takes place.

(2) A person who intentionally assists in the suicide of another person or procures for that other person the means to commit suicide, is liable to a term of imprisonment of not more than three years or a fine of the fourth category (€ 21,750[35]) if the suicide takes place. Article 293 sub 2 is applicable accordingly.

3.2.3.2. Main amendments in the Burial and Cremation Act

Art. 7 Burial and Cremation Act as amended by the Law on Euthanasia reads:

(1) A person who performed an autopsy shall issue a death certificate if he or she is convinced that the death occurred by a natural cause.

(2) If the death was the result of the application of termination of life on request or assisted suicide as referred to in art. 293 sub (2) or art. 294 sub (2) Criminal Code, the attending physician shall not issue a death certificate and shall immediately notify the municipal autopsist or one of the municipal autopsists of the cause of death by completing a form. The physician shall supplement this form with a reasoned report with respect to the due observance of the requirements of due care referred to in art. 2 of the Termination of Life on Request and Assisted Suicide (Review Procedures) Act.

(3) If the attending physician believes in other cases than referred to sub (2) that he may not issue a death certificate, he must immediately notify the municipal autopsist or one of the municipal autopsists of this fact by completing a form.

Art. 9 sub (1) of the Burial and Cremation Act provides that the form and the set-up of the models of the death certificate shall be laid down by order in council. Like wise the set-up of models of notification and all the necessary reports must be prepared.

For the report referred to in art. 7 sub (2), the notification referred to in art. 7 sub (3) and the forms referred to in art. 10 (notification of the municipal autopsist to the public prosecutor, the registrar of birth, death, and marriages) shall be provided by order in council. There are also forms in use for the reports of the

---

34 Since 1.1.2020, before: € 20,500.
35 Since 1.1.2020, before: € 20,500.

municipal autopsist to the regional review committees referred to in art. 3 of the Termination of Life on Request and Assisted Suicide (Review Procedures) Act.

3.3. The Review Procedures step by step

(1) A physician terminated the life of a person on his or her express and earnest request or assisted a person committing suicide.

(2) He reports this as unnatural death to the municipal autopsist and adds a declaration giving the reasons why the termination of life in this case met the requirements of due care, the report of the physician(s) he/she consulted and other documents, for example, a written volition concerning euthanasia.

(3) The municipal autopsist does a post-mortem, controls how life was terminated, controls the documents, contacts the public prosecutor who makes up a declaration of no objections whereafter the registrar of births, deaths, and marriages can permit the burial or cremation. Finally, the autopsist sends the documents to the Regional Review Committee Euthanasia.

(4) When the Regional Review Committee receives the documents, it registers all relevant facts, and an experienced secretary makes an evaluation whether the report shall lead to questions by the committee or not. The secretary composes a draft opinion that is sent together with the documents to the members of the committee.

(5) Those cases that do not cause any further questions are generally viewed digitally. If there are questions, these are formulated in written and the physician is asked to answer them by e-mail or fax to settle the cases as quickly as possible.

(6) The cases that led to questions are settled during the monthly meetings of the Review Committee. Depending on the questions that rise, the committee can collect further information by telephone or by inviting the physician to give further information before the committee. This generally has place in all cases in which the committee is about to conclude that the physician did not meet the required due care.

(7) The Review Committee generally decides the cases within 6 weeks after the report was received. If the committee concludes that the physician did not act in accordance with due care the committee generally invites the physician so that he is able to give important additional information before the committee decides once and for all.

(8) If the committee concludes "not in accordance with due care" this means that the physician did not act in accordance with the legal regulations. The

committee is obliged to send this judgement together with all documents to the Procurators General and the Inspection for Public Health. The committee also informs the medical doctor directly about the decision taken.

(9) If the committee concludes that the medical doctor acted with due care, which means that he acted according to the legal regulations, this is a final decision. The Review Committee informs the physician in written about this decision.

(10) The Procurators General and the Inspection of Public Health finally decide according to their own competence and responsibility.

In connection with the Dutch Review Procedure a regulation proposed in the Portuguese and Spanish bills to decriminalize euthanasia and assisted suicide[36] is of special interest. In contrast to the Dutch regulation, here a request for euthanasia must be agreed by a specially established review commission already **in advance**. Without a permission of the review commission, euthanasia and assisted suicide may not take place. A review after euthanasia or assisted suicide then only concerns the questions of due care. Such a regulation offers the physicians more, respectively the wanted, certainty as they know already before they end the life of a patient that the appropriate authority generally agrees.

What concerns the contents of the Spanish and the Portuguese regulations, they are rather similar and a bit stricter than the Dutch one.[37]

3.4. Euthanasia and Dementia

The most difficult cases of requests for euthanasia are those of patients suffering from dementia. Their suffering is hopeless because the illness is progressive and not curable, but their suffering is often difficult to determine and the question in how far their will is independent is - if at all - not easy to answer. Only **in 2004,** thus after the Law on Euthanasia came into force in 2002, the first case of euthanasia of a patient suffering from dementia was reported by a Review Committee. **In 2015,** there were already 109 of these cases reported and they all were accepted by the Review Committees, some of them even in cases of advanced dementia, in which however a certain possibility to communicate was still present.[38]

---

36 A. Hendriks, Euthanasie in Zuid-Europa, Nederlands Juristenblad (NJB) 2020, p. 1735, 1738.

37 A. Hendriks, Euthanasie in Zuid-Europa, NJB 2020, p. 1736-1739.

38 Jaarverslag RTE (Regionale Toetsingscommissie Euthanasie/ Regional Review Commission Euthanasia) 2015.

Against cases of advanced dementia in which the patient is no longer able to realize what happens most physicians and the Royal Dutch Medical Association have rather strong moral aversions. In January 2016, a Review Committee reported that they were informed about such a case in which the patient obviously did not understand what was happening and the physician according to their opinion did not act with due care.[39] The publication of this case resulted on the 9th of February 2017 in a big advertisement in one of the main Dutch newspapers, NRC/Handelsblad, in which 220 medical doctors lodged together their moral objections against the killing of a helpless human being.[40]

Important for the medical doctors is in those cases that the patient at the end of his life still has the will to choose euthanasia. Therefore, a declaration of this will in written in earlier times has for many of them only little significance. Furthermore, it is rather important to know that not only physicians in general but also geriatricians with their special knowledge about elderly people have great problems with euthanasia for people suffering from advanced dementia.[41]

3.5. Evaluations of the Law on Euthanasia

3.5.1. Introduction

In the Netherlands it is since many years usual to evaluate how legal regulations are practiced, what their effects are, what their effectiveness is like and whether amendments of the law or the development of guidelines for practice are needed. The Law on Euthanasia was evaluated already three times, the first time in 2007[42], in 2011[43] and then in 2017.[44]

---

39 www.euthanasiecommissie.nl/publicaties/oordelen/2016.

40 NRC/Handelsblad, daily newspaper, 10-02-2017.

41 B. Chabot, De euthanasiegeest is uit de fles, NRC/ Handelsblad, 18-06-2017, opinie en debat, p. 4/5.

42 D.B. Onwuteaka-Philipsen et al., Evaluatie WTL (Wet Toetsing Levensbeëindiging op verzoek en hulp bij zelfdoding), ZonMw (Nederlandse Organisatie voor gezondheidsonderzoek en zorginnovatie), Den Haag, 2007.

43 A. van der Heide et al., Tweede evaluatie Wet Levensbeëindiging op verzoek en hulp bij zelfdoding. Reeks evaluatie regelgeving, deel 33, Den Haag, ZonMw, 2012.

44 Kamerstukken (Parliamentary Documents) II 2016/2017. 31 036, nr. 9.

3.5.2. General findings 2011

The overall conclusion of the second evaluation was that the Law on Euthanasia has succeeded in improving the carefulness of medical doctors who terminate the life of a patient upon his or her request and in offering a transparent and consistent legal framework for practice.[45]

3.5.3. Some important results of the evaluations 2011 and 2017

As we cannot discuss these long evaluation reports here in detail we only focus on some important results and views concerning

1) subjects until now here more or less neglected, as there are, the performance of euthanasia, psychiatric diagnoses, "weary of life", the "End-of-life-Clinic" and
2) important subjective opinions of medical doctors interviewed in connection with the evaluations.

Ad 1) The practice of the review committees was studied among other methods by an analysis of 316 files of cases dating from 2011 and resulted in the statement that the review processes proved to be rather uniform and consistent. The only requirement of due care that caused some inconsistencies was the one concerning the careful performance of euthanasia. The opinions of the members of the Review Committees vary in so far for example concerning the way in which medication was administered, the duration of the procedure and how the depth of the patient's coma is checked before the administration of muscle relaxants. This finding at the same time gives an idea about how detailed the reviews are.

During recent years, the belief that termination of life can also be an option for patients with dementia, psychiatric diagnoses or many simultaneous geriatric complaints at the same time is slowly gaining influence among the physicians and the members of the Review Committees and in this way a more liberal opinion grew. Anyhow, the number of reported cases of this kind increased but is still small. While in 2008 there were only two cases with a psychiatric diagnosis reported and accepted in 2015 there were 56 and in 2016 altogether 60 of them.[46] The question whether these patients can give informed consent or not is a big problem. Therefore, an independent psychiatrist must regularly be involved in these cases and asked for advise (see the Case Chabot above).

---

45 A. van der Heide et al., see above.
46 E. Pans, 15 jaar Euthanasiewet Ars Aequi 2017, p. 273 and following.

The basis for a more liberal attitude was the Law on Euthanasia itself with its "open standards" which made it possible that new views and opinions that developed in society became influential with practitioners via adequate new interpretations of the law and a corresponding application of the legal rules. The main reason for these developments seems to be the growing of knowledge in practice. The "End-of-Life-Clinic" (see below) plays an important role so far as it is generally seen as the expertise center to decide on "the complex cases".[47] Furthermore the publication of the Code of Practice of the Regional Review Committees Euthanasia (RTE) is a great help in refining the standards of euthanasia.[48] In this Code, summarized per type of request, one can read what the actual requirements for the request in question are.

The same development towards a more liberal opinion can be found in connection with the so-called "weary of life" cases. The Royal Dutch Medical Association issued a guideline on this topic in 2011, that shows that there already exists an agreement that the scope of the medical-professional domain is more extended than was commonly assumed on basis of the Brongersma verdict of the Supreme Court in 2002, see above.[49]

The "End-of-Life-Clinic", founded in 2012, aims to help patients who cannot find a physician who is willing to terminate their life although the requirements of due care are present. Euthanasia is not a duty for a medical doctor. He is not obliged to act according to any request. If he is not willing to comply with the request, he regularly will refer the patient to a colleague.

For patients with a complex request the End-of-Life-Clinic often is their last hope, but also here not every request is accepted. In 2015 "only" 31% of these cases were agreed.[50] The End-of-Life-Clinic has ambulant teams with one physician and one nurse each working in each region.

In 2016 and 2017 the End-of Life-Clinic received much more requests than it could handle as its capacity (59 medical doctors and 6 psychiatrists) was not big enough. Regarding the number of requests there were by then already double as many physicians needed. The main reason for the big number of requests is that many physicians and psychiatrist do not dare to decide on the requests of their own patients but refer them to the End-of-Life-Clinic. This practice is heavily criticized by the End-of-Life-Clinic. As there are at present not enough

---

47 www.levenseindekliniek.nl; at present: Center of Expertise Euthanasia
48 E. Pans, see above.
49 A. van de Heide et al., above.
50 E. Pans, above, p. 278.

psychiatrists working at this clinic, mainly psychiatric patients often must wait for months before their case can be decided. Furthermore, it would be much better if the psychiatrist who treated the patient would decide the case himself.

Ad 2) In the following some of the results of the questionnaire study conducted under general practitioners, clinical specialists and nursing home physicians that concern important subjective opinions of medical doctors are summarized:

> The annual number of patients asking their medical doctor for euthanasia grew from 6,7% of all deaths in 2010 to 8,4% of all deaths in 2015. The percentage of agreed requests grew the same time from 45% to 55%.

Of all Dutch physicians 85% is willing to provide euthanasia upon a patient's request in cases of hopeless suffering. About 42% of the physicians are willing to help patients in cases of beginning dementia when they are still able to give informed consent but only 16% are willing to help those patients who are suffering without a serious medical reason being "weary of life".

Most of the physicians think that they can provide adequate palliative care. They do not believe that further improving the quality of palliative care would make euthanasia redundant.

The frequency of using continuous deep sedation at the end of life has increased. Sometimes medical doctors prefer continuous deep sedation as means to alleviate suffering in respect to euthanasia.

A bit less than half of the physicians is convinced that voluntarily stopping eating and drinking can be a reasonable alternative for euthanasia.

3.6. Results of the introduction of the Law on Euthanasia

Since the Law on Euthanasia came into force the number of euthanasia cases grew from 1,815 accepted cases in 2002 to 5,516 in 2015, and 6,100 in 2016.[51] During these 15 years since the Law on Euthanasia came into force, the number of cases reported to the Review Committees got triple as many and the end of the growth is not yet in sight.[52] However, meanwhile (2020) it became obvious that the number of cases is not always steadily growing. From 2017 to 2018, for example, there was a decrease from 6,585 to 6,126 cases. In 2019 the number increased again (6,361 cases) but did not reach the number registered in 2017.

---

51 Jaarverslag RTE (Regional Review Commission Euthanasia 2015, p. 7, NRC/Handelsblad, 23-06-2017, p. 2; www.dutchnews.nl 2021/04.

52 E. Pans, above, p. 273.

An important reason for the all over increase of euthanasia cases might be the fact that the present generation of elderly people is less religious, has more longings for and insight in their rights of self-determination, more knowledge about their rights as patients and is in general more independent and able to be responsible for their own life than the old population about some decennia before.[53] Another important reason might be that physicians meanwhile noticed that with the introduction of the Law on Euthanasia, criminal law was placed more in the distance.

Cases of accepted requests for euthanasia concern for the biggest part patients with a terminal illness who only have a short time to live. Through the years about 75% of these people had cancer, in 2015 for example 4,000 of the 5,516 requests were based on cancer, followed by 311 cases of illnesses of the nervous system and 233 cases of heart- and vascular diseases.[54] These cases in which the physicians help their patients in emergency situations are widely accepted in public and by the Review Committees.

3.7. The latest Ministerial Order about prosecution decisions concerning active termination of life on request of the Department of Prosecution of the 17th of May 2017

Until the new Order came into force, the Department of Public Prosecutors needed the permission of the Minister of Security and Justice, meanwhile the Minister of Justice and Security, to prosecute a medical doctor who did not act with due care in cases of euthanasia. According to the new Order decisions to prosecute or not physicians in connection with the articles 293 and 294 Criminal Code must be still characterized as very delicate matters, but the Procurators General no longer need the permission of the Minister but just must report these cases to him. In this way the new Order strengthens the position of the Department of Public Prosecution in this area.

Furthermore, in this Order two of the requirements of due care in art. 2 Law on Euthanasia were marked as substantial. These are the demands that

1) the physician is convinced that the request of the patient is the result of his/ her own free will and well considered
2) the suffering of the patient is hopeless, and unbearable.

---

53 E. Pans, above, p. 273.
54 Jaarverslag RTE 2015, p. 10.

If one of these two requirements is not complied with, prosecution is principally indicated. In the other cases the Prosecutors-General can drop prosecution or choose a conditional dismissal.[55]

This latest Order can make things concerning the present prosecution policies clearer for the Prosecution Service, but also for the physicians.

4. The State of Affairs in 2017

4.1. Introduction

In 2017 the so-called **pill of Drion** was discussed again in the Netherlands in connection with what is named "completed life", formerly described as suffering by living, ready with life, or ready to leave life, a condition of old people who are not ill, do not suffer extremely but are only tired of life and would like to have the pill of Drion at their disposal.

Who was Drion? Huib Drion was an important Dutch jurist, among other things a well-known writer, professor of private law at Leyden University, and later Justice at the Supreme Court in The Hague.

In 1991 he published an article in NRC/Handelsblad,[56] one of the most important Dutch newspapers, titled "The self-chosen end of elderly people" in which he proposed a hypothetic pill for old people with which they get the possibility to end their life in a humanely manner at a time self-chosen without the help of a physician. The idea was that the pill should be available under certain security conditions freely for people 75 years of age and older that existed of two portions, pill A and pill B to use with an interval of some days so that there would be time to reconsider. The discussion Drion provoked, was that about the right to commit suicide, according to his opinion a Human Right. Drion developed this proposal principally starting from the insight that the possibility to have a pill as this at one's disposal would offer many old people more peace and rest during their further life. A thought that many people agreed with as most reactions of the readers of Drion's article made obvious. Drion died in 2004 shortly before his 87th birthday in his sleep.

Els Borst by then Minister of Public Health for the left liberal D'66 caused in reaction of Drion's article upheaval in the Netherlands by stating that she would like to legalize the pill of Drion.

---

55 Kamerstukken (Parliamentary Documents) II 2016/2017, 32 647, nr. 67.
56 NRC/Handelsblad, 19-10-1991, Het zelfgewilde einde van oudere mensen.

4.2. The discussion on "The Right to Commit Suicide" in recent years

As was already stated above the Supreme Court stipulated in **2002** in connection with the Case Brongersma that only in cases classified as medical was it possible to refer to the Law on Euthanasia. Meanwhile, however, the Review Committees also accepted a combination of several different geriatric complaints at the same time as a reason for unbearable hopeless suffering.[57]

In **2016** an Advisory Committee, a so-called committee of wise persons, worked on the question how to develop broader juridical regulations granting more self-determination for the individual elderly people, at the same time caring for their security as well as for their protection and preventing the abuse of the regulation.[58] The Commission concluded that it was not possible to create a regulation that at the same time meets all these needs sufficiently and added the warning not to impair the principles of the Law on Euthanasia.

Again, the courts cleared the state of affairs: **The Case Heringa**
In **2008**, Albert Heringa assisted his 99 years old stepmother to commit suicide. She did not want to live any more because her life had become meaningless for her. The court in Zutphen found him guilty but did not impose a punishment. The public prosecutor appealed. The court of appeal in Arnhem concluded, that the special circumstances of the case made it possible to accept the existence of a state of emergency and found Heringa therefore not liable to punishment.[59] The public prosecutor filed a cassation with the Supreme Court.

The Supreme Court stated, however, that the demands of due care in the Law on Euthanasia are strongly combined with the expert knowledge of the medical profession and that therefore a not-physician can only in special exceptional cases refer to circumstances beyond his control. This decision corresponds to the ratio of the Law on Euthanasia that is principally meant to address physicians. The Supreme Court was not convinced that in the case of Heringa such a special exception was given and referred the case back to the court of appeal in Den Bosch, where the public prosecutor acknowledged that Heringa's motives were pure, but only doctors may assist with suicides. The prosecutor demanded

---

57 Jaarverslag RTE 2015, p. 31-32.
58 Adviescommissie Voltooid Leven, voorzitter: P. Schnabel, Den Haag 2016.
59 ECLI:NL GHARI: 2915: 3444 (Heringa).

a three-months suspended prison sentence against Heringa. The final decision was in 2017 not taken.[60]

4.3. A new draft-bill

"The completed life" problem is also an important subject in the discussion of politicians, and it was again the left-liberal party D'66 that prepared a draft bill[61] that was planned to be discussed in parliament after a new government would have been formed and installed after the elections of the 15th of March **2017**. The idea was, to place a **Completed Life Law** next to the Law on Euthanasia. Until the end of August 2017, the deadline of this **Part 1**, the formation of a new government did not take place.

In the concept of D'66, persons were introduced who have the task to accompany those at the end of their life who feel and are convinced that their life is "completed". For this task not only physicians but also nurses, psychologists specialized in medical care or psychotherapists can be chosen according to the concept bill. However, regarding how difficult the task of accompanying the last phase of life is, one cannot be sure that the proposed professionals dispose of the right and sufficient education and training for this work, to which it belongs to test the soundness of mind, to find out whether there were influences or even pressures from third persons, to inform whether there are possibilities to change the facts that cause the wish to terminate life and finally accompanying the termination of life.[62]

According to the opinion of the Royal Dutch Medical Association the proposed Completed Life Law is a concept easily to sympathize with, but there are too many risks, such as the risk that old people will feel unsafe or become stigmatized and that the slowly developed practice of euthanasia erodes.

The concept bill proposes that the persons who are involved in the **"End of Life Accompanying"** should get a special education and should be controlled by special commissions comparable with the Review Committees and by the regular disciplinary tribunals of the Health Service.

Whether the content of this draft bill is what people want who after earnest consideration concluded that their life is "definitely" completed, is as much

---

60 See for the continuation of the proceedings at the court of appeal in Den Bosch and the final judgement below Part 2.3.
61 https://d66.nl/content/uploads/sites/2/2016/12/ Wet-toetsing-levensbeëindiging-van ouderen op verzoek.
62 E. Pans, above, p. 281.

doubtful as whether the proposed regulation can sufficiently guarantee the protection of the rights of these people. However, this concept bill can be a starting point for new serious considerations and discussions that are obviously necessary as the subject keeps so many people busy at present and there is a possibility that a regulation is found that offers a better compromise between the conflicting interests of the free will of the mature responsible individual and the safety and dignity of individuals and society.

4.4. The Dutch Society for Psychiatry

In 2017 the Dutch Society for Psychiatry (NVvP) gave its opinion on the practice of psychiatrics to refer those of their patients who ask for euthanasia to the End-of-Life-Clinic instead of taking a decision themselves. The commission of the NVvP that is developing guidelines for practicing euthanasia stated that it is a very undesirable situation that psychiatrists refer their patients for reasons of acting shyness[63] to the End-of-Life-Clinic. The psychiatrists must investigate themselves the requests of their patients and fulfill them if all preconditions are present. This is an important new vision.

5. Final remarks 2017

For the presentation of the regulation of Euthanasia in the Netherland the historical structure was chosen intentionally. This structure shows very well that the legislator acted slowly and thoroughly and was guided by the facts and by the time. The development of the Law on Euthanasia is a good example how the Dutch develop their law by using methods of the social sciences, not at least regular evaluation studies. Legislation without following evaluation studies is rather seldom in connection with highly controversial subjects in the Netherlands. In this way one tries to meet the responsibility towards society.

The present regulation of euthanasia in the Netherlands is **not a decriminalization in the narrow sense** of the word. The termination of human life on request and assisted suicide are still punishable. Under the condition that the by and by in practice developed, meanwhile rather clearly defined requirements of due care were fulfilled, it is possible to refrain from punishment. This possibility was developed in court practice in the framework of the principle of expediency and got a special legal basis with the introduction of the Law on Euthanasia in 2002 in the shape of a criminal defence.

---

63   E. van Steenbergen, NRC/Handelsblad, 27-10-2017 p. 1.

In **2017**, the Law on Euthanasia was in force since more than 15 years. It was already evaluated three times then, and overall, the review was positive. This, however, was not a reason for the various pressure groups, communities of interest and other organizations, the media, political parties etc. to stop discussions as by far neither, all their ideas were realized, nor their aims completely reached, and all their aspirations fulfilled. The discussion about the question whether euthanasia should be allowed in connection with advanced dementia and psychiatric diseases burst out just recently again and there lies already a new bill about a Law on Completed Life prepared by Pia Dijkstra, member of the Lower House for the left-wing Liberal Party D'66.

As it seemed in 2017, the new Dutch government became a coalition of the right- and the left-wing Liberal Parties VVD and D'66 and two small Christian parties, the Christian Democratic Appel, a Party with members of different Christian churches (Protestants and Catholics) and the Christian Union of orthodox protestant signature. Both Christian parties being heavy opponents of a Law on Completed Life.

According to the designed Minister of Health Edith Schippers (VVD), parliament already in 2017 was convinced that the present Law on Euthanasia offers "people with advanced dementia and psychiatric patients" the possibility to "get euthanasia if all due care requirements are fulfilled".[64]

For what concerns the Law on a Completed Life it was still in **2020** difficult to predict when it will be ready and what its content will be. The discussion not yet really started, and it will become a heavy and hot one. Looking back on the long history of the development of the present legislation on euthanasia it is not at all far fetched to think that one is choosing for a learning by doing again and just waits, what the future judgments will be before one decides on the content of the bill and the time of introduction for a Law on "Completed Life". The Dutch legal system is elastic enough to make this possible.

Looking back to our **Preface** where we summed up the ideas that were current on euthanasia in antiquity, we could conclude in 2017[65], that individual full citizens in those old days had more rights to decide on their own life than we nowadays have in our enlightened free societies, which boast to guarantee human dignity but prevent people who are no longer physically and or psychically able to live with dignity according to their own opinion, to die at least worthily.

---

64 E. Schippers, NRC/Handelsblad, 23-6-2017, p. 2.
65 And can still conclude at the end of 2021.

This finding gives rise to the question about the reason for this difference between the old days and our times. Why is the will of the individual nowadays not decisive when it is about the termination of life? And is this reason, respectively if there are more of them, are these reasons really in harmony with presently generally in public accepted views?

Part 2 The development from 2017 until the end of 2021

1. Introduction

At the time, the 2017 report on "Euthanasia in the Netherlands" was completed, presented in Greece, and published in Portugal[66], there still was no new government installed in the Netherlands. After the elections of the 15th of March 2017, it was extremely difficult to form a coalition and accordingly it took even longer than any time before since the end of World War II, about 7 months, until the coalition agreement 2017-2021 was ready. This agreement got the hopeful title "Trust in the Future". The new government, the third under Prime Minister Rutte (Rutte III) finally became a coalition of the right-wing liberals (VVD), the left-wing liberals (D'66), the Christian Democratic Union (CDA), and the Christian Union. Almost every council of ministers based on a coalition has certain subjects for which it is simply impossible to find a compromise. For Rutte III the extent of freedom for individuals to decide about the end of their own life was such a topic. In the coalition agreement 2017-2020[67] this reads as follows: 'Where opinions are dominated by philosophy of life, belief, persuasion, ideals and conscience, there can not be demanded to abandon these principles. The coalition agreement shows a way to handle differences of this kind respectfully'.

The best thing one could do under the existing circumstances - and in the Netherlands this option is generally used - is just to accept the differences and postpone decisions in positions of stalemate at least temporarily. It is a rather easy, at the same time usually effective and at any rate elegant way of acting for the present. To stimulate further developments nevertheless actively, the time of

---

66 In Portugal, the manuscript "Euthanasia and Suicide in Dutch Law" was translated between 2017 and 2021 in three parts parallel with its time of origin by Manuela Baptista Lopes, until 2018 senior adviser in the Portuguese Constitutional Court, Lisbon: Eutanásia na Holanda: A evolução da actual regulamentação jurídica, sua prática e um novo projecto de lei-quadro. Revista do Ministério Público 152: Outubro: Dezembro 2017 [pp. 93-134].
Continuation 2021: Quando o próprio tira a vida a si mesmo – Eutanásia e suicídio na lei holandesa. Revista do Ministério Público 166: Abril: Junho 2021 [pp. 215-255] and Suicídio e eutanásia à luz dos direitos à vida e à autodeterminação. Revista do Ministério Público 167: Julho: Setembro 2021 [pp. 149-204].

67 Regeerakkoord 2017-2021, 10-10-2017, p. 17.

standstill is in similar situations used for additional research and broad discussions in society.

2. The coalition agreement 2017–2021

In the coalition agreement 2017, the coalition partners stressed that medical science should have the possibility for research and to practice the results found to overcome illness, to prevent unnecessary suffering and to improve quality of life. Already in the next sentence attention is paid to the existing important restrictions for medical science under Rutte III as there are valid legal and other regulations with their ethical dimensions. As far as it concerns political decisions in connection with the adjustment or modification of the present law, the coalition agreement declares that the council of ministers surely will only do so, if the convincing of all political parties participating in the coalition were taken into consideration, and the following three questions were sufficiently answered:

1) Is the extension of the research - and application possibilities really a medical scientific necessity or are there other alternatives that need less policy space?
2) What is the medical-ethical dimension and what the Health Council of the Netherlands and other advisory bodies already stated so far?
3) Did a social discussion take place already and was there sufficient political reflection? [68]

Accordingly, the new government was not willing to introduce a Bill on Completed Life in parliament, but the left-wing liberals got the possibility to introduce their initiative law in parliament.

The coalition agreement 2017 until about spring 2021 refers to the results of the Commission Schnabel that concluded in 2016 that the current legislation offers already more possibilities than medical doctors seem to notice and that the number of people who cannot be helped in the frame of the present "Termination of Life on Request and Assisted Suicide Law"[69] seems to be rather low. Furthermore, the coalition agreement pointed out, that as well proponents as opponents of a "Completed Life Law" stress the importance of a broad discussion in public and a diligent approach to the topic.

Furthermore, the coalition agreement 2017 until the end of 2020 announced the following steps:

---

68 Regeerakkoord 2017-2021, p. 17.
69 WTL or wtl (euthanasie).

1) The council of ministers shall start to execute the advices given by the manifesto "Aging with Dignity", which was initiated by Gert-Jan Segers, group chairman of the Christian Union in parliament, Jan Slagter, director broadcaster MAX, a Dutch broadcaster focussing on people aged 50 years and older, and Manon van der Kaa, director Catholic Interests Association Elderly (KBO), an organisation for and by seniors, working for a society in which seniors have a full place.

2) The Minister of Health shall focus on the results of the Commission Schnabel again and on the results of the third evaluation of the "Termination of Life on Request and Assisted Suicide Law"[70].

3) Research shall be initiated focussing on the extent and the circumstances of the people who according to the results of the Commission Schnabel believe not to be helped sufficiently by the "Termination of Life on Request and Assisted Suicide Law". The council of ministers will decide what consequences the research results should have and offers the parliament the possibility to prepare initiative legislation.

3. Continuation and final judgment of the Heringa Case

After Rutten III was installed, the Heringa Case was for the 4th and 5th time in court.

The prosecutor of the court of appeal in Den Bosch demanded, as already reported above, a three-months suspended prison sentence against Heringa.[71] The court of appeal in Den Bosch, however, ruled that Heringa was guilty of assisted suicide and could not invoke force majeure. Surely there had been possibilities for Heringa to find the help of a doctor after the family doctor had refused to help his stepmother. The court further specially emphasized the two facts, that Heringa left his mother alone after she had taken the deadly mixture and that he did not immediately tell what had happened.

The fact that Heringa made a video of all that happened during euthanasia was conducted, including the conversation he had with his stepmother, is difficult to judge. The video was shown on the 8th of February 2010 in a documentary titled "The last wish of mum ('Moek'). A self-directed death", broadcasted in the programme "Netwerk"[72]. There are different interpretations possible.

---

70 See above Part 1, 3.5.
71 See above Part 1, 4.2.
72 Supreme Court, 16-04-2019 ECLI: NL:2019:598.

Without being precisely informed about what Heringa's motives and reasons so far were and whether his stepmother was informed about and had agreed with the publication of the video, one can only guess. Anyhow, after this broadcast, the criminal proceedings began.

Finally, the court of appeal in Den Bosch on the 31st of **January 2018** imposed 6 months conditional prison sentence, three months more than the prosecutor had demanded, with an operational period of 2 years.[73]

The judgment caused a lot of discussions in public and several organisations, one of them, the Royal Dutch Medical Association, offered Heringa support.

Heringa brought an appeal to the Supreme Court, mainly stating the fact that he could not invoke force majeure. In his advice, the Advocate General declared that there were no grounds to set the judgement of the court of appeal aside. The Supreme Court came to the same conclusion, stating that according to Dutch law, euthanasia may generally only be performed by medical doctors and only in special cases by somebody without this qualification. The Heringa Case, however, did not belong to these exceptional cases, a fact, according to the opinion of the Supreme Court, the court of appeal had sufficiently motivated. Therefore, the judgment of the court of appeal in Den Bosch had to continue to exist.[74]

4. The "Perspective Research"

Perspectives on the wish to die of people being 55 years of age and older, not being seriously ill: The people and the figures[75]

4.1. Introduction

The research was initiated on basis of the **coalition agreement 2017-2021** and executed on behalf of the Ministry of Health by Els van Wijngaarden et al.[76]

---

73 ECLI:NL:GHSHE: 2018:345.

74 Supreme Court (Hoge Raad der Nederlanden) ECLI:NL:2019:598, www.rechtspraak. nl/Organisatie-en-contact/Organisatie/Hoge-Raad-der-Nederlanden/Nieuws/Paginas/Veroordeling-Heringa-wegens-bieden-van-hulp-bij-zelfdoding-moeder-blijft-in-stand.aspx .

75 Els van Wijngaarden et al., The Perspective Report, Research of the University of Humanistic Studies Utrecht and the University Medical Centre Utrecht on behalf of the Dutch Ministry of Health, Den Haag, ZonMw, January 2020.

76 Els van Wijngaarden et al., 2020.

Els van Wijngaarden is a Master of religious studies who recently wrote a thesis with the title "Completed Life, About Living and the Wish to Die"[77]. Her ethical work is based mainly on the life experiences of respondents and a result of the application of a combination of several scientific disciplines, mainly care ethics, gerontology, and death studies. These disciplines determine the basic principles, the range of research, and the extent of the results of her study.

The research commissioned by the Ministry of Health primarily concerned the question, whether, respectively in how far, the completed life concept is in harmony with reality. It aimed at finding answers to the following questions:

(1) To whom does the Euthanasia Law 2001 offer no adequate help?
(2) How big is this group?
(3) What are the living conditions and circumstances of these people?

The research was divided into

(1) a study of the existing relevant literature and of the application of the Law on Euthanasia 2001 in practice,
(2) quantitative research with questionnaires for people aged 55 years and older and for medical doctors, and
(3) qualitative research with in-depth interviews with persons who had participated in the quantitative part of the research and a longitudinal analysis of interviews which took place respectively in the years 2013, 2017 and 2019.

In the following the focus is limited to the main results of the quantitative and the qualitative studies.

4.2. The quantitative research

It was for the first time in Dutch history that the number of generally healthy people with a wish to die and to end their lives was registered. There were **32,477** questionnaires spread under inhabitants aged 55 years and older. **21,294** people answered. Forty-four percent of these respondents were 55–64 years of age, 39% 65–74 years, and 17% were 75 years and older.

Of the **8,381** medical doctors (general practitioners) who received a questionnaire, not more than **1,637** gave a response.[78]

---

77 Voltooid Leven, over leven en willen sterven, Atlas Contact, 2016, ISBN 9789045033044.
78 Els van Wijngaarden et al., p. 11.

4.2.1. The 21,294 interviewees aged 55 years and older

Of the interviewed people of 55 years and older, **1.25%** had a persistent desire to die although they were not seriously ill. Partly their desire was passive in the sense, that so far, they had no concrete plans.[79] Although the respondents of this group declared not to be seriously ill, many of them reported important health problems and behaved in a way that made the existence of a light or moderate depression rather probable. Therefore, this group can not really be categorized as "healthy". 19% of this group stated that they had the wish to die already lifelong. However, for most of them - 72% - this desire was not continuously dominant. 45% of the group declared that during the last week the wish to live and the wish to be dead were equally strong. 70% of the group answered the question how they would describe their death wish with "a desire for a natural death" or "a desire not to wake up tomorrow".[80]

Among the group with a death wish, there were relatively more people with a negative look back to the past, a negative evaluation of the present and negative expectations of the future.

Important factors the seniors related to their death wish were often worrying (65%), the feeling to have no or little influence on life, loneliness, physical, and mental senile decay, but also financial problems (26%) and the seasons (22%) were mentioned, whereas as positive, the wish to live strengthening factors they chose primarily a nice home (67%), but also independence, calm, to matter for others, a feeling of freedom, humour and/or pleasure and respect and appreciation of others.[81]

For the question what their necessities were, 47% answered with the wish to have a means to commit suicide at their disposal and 25% to get the help of a medical doctor. Furthermore, better understanding, more financial means, good conversations with a relief worker and more social contacts were the main answers.

0.73% of the respondents answered that they had an **active will** and already had started to make plans or to prepare such an act, for example by becoming a member of an adequate interest organisation or by starting with the reduction of treatment.

---

79 Els van Wijngaarden et al., p. 12.
80 Els van Wijngaarden et al., p. 12.
81 Els van Wijngaarden et al., p. 13.

To this group with an active death wish belonged people of all life categories participating in the research.

One third of them was low educated, half of them belonged to the lower social classes, one quarter had no children, half of them was living alone and more than the half was living in a city. These demographic characteristics were similar those of the group with a passive desire to die. People with an active wish to die had as well important health problems as symptoms of depression.

People with an active desire to die significantly more often thought about death. Intensifying factors for their death wish were illness, restrictions of freedom, depending on others, feelings to have no or only little influence on their own life and to be a burden for others, worrying, financial problems, and the seasons. What concerned the positive factors, the wish to live strengthening factors, there were no differences found between the people with an active and those with a passive wish to die.

People with an active wish to die relatively more often were longing for means to commit suicide (55% in relation to 35%) and more often needed more financial means (23% versus 12%).

Respondents with a **passive death wish** less often asked for help in connection with their intended suicide (16% versus 7%).

To find out the number of people that probably would make use of a legal regulation of help in cases of suicide, the research also focused on the group of people aged 55 years and more with an **active death wish, and the intention to end life**. This group existed of 36 persons or 0.17 % of the sample of 21,294 respondents.

67% of this group were female and 44% were low educated. There were less religious people in the group with a wish to end life (29%) than in the whole group of persons with a persistent wish for death (37%). The percentages of people without children and living alone were a bit lower than among the whole group with a persistent death wish. People with the desire to end life were more often living in or near a city and more often living in the province South-Holland, where the population density is relatively high.

The group respondents with a death wish and the intention to end life reported about the same health problems as the bigger group of the respondents with just a death wish.

As the factors intensifying the wish to end life often were reported worrying (81%), physical and mental senile decay (61%), loneliness (56%), feelings not to have influence on the own life anymore (50%), illness (47%), restriction of freedom and being a burden for others (47%). Mainly worrying and financial problems were relatively more often reported by those with the intention to die.

Quite interesting were two of the three most often chosen positive factors of the group with a death wish: independence (69%) and feelings of freedom (67%). The third positive factor was with also 69% a nice home.

67% of the group with a death wish wanted to have information about means to end life oneself, 42% preferred the help of a medical doctor. Both percentages are higher than in the group with an active desire to die.

In the Netherlands ca. 1,700 people aged 75 years and older have a very concrete wish to die; however, also among them, there are cases in which the wish to live will finally win.

Calculating the number of people with an active desire to die among the total Dutch population based on the research results found by Els van den Wijngaarden et al., their number is about 10,156 people of 55 years and older, respectively about 0.18% of the total Dutch population.

4.2.2. The interviewed medical practitioners

There were 1,144 questionnaires filled in by medical practitioners. A quarter of the doctors stated that there were no people aged 55 years and older who thought to have no future and had the wish to die while not being ill. 44% of the doctors reported a percentage between 0.1% and 1%. Half of the doctors thus estimated that in a "normal practice" with 2095 patients, there are less than 2 patients with the respective problem.

The persons the medical practitioners described were mainly 85–89 years old. In 73% of the cases, they were female. In 55% of the cases the individuals were tired of existing and in 46% lonely. Furthermore, the loss of the partner and/of physical and mental functions with their consequences - social isolation, no longer being able to read the newspaper and to be engaged in hobbies - were important reasons.

The medical practitioners described the death wish of these people in 64% of the cases with, 'no more waking up in the morning and dying during sleep'.

About 46% of the family doctors reported that the respective people wanted their help, not immediately but in future.[82]

---

82 Els van Wijngaarden et al., p. 15.

4.3. The qualitative research

4.3.1. Introduction

The Qualitative Research also had two sections. Firstly, there were 34 in-depth interviews initiated with seniors who took already part in the quantitative research and who experienced that they had (1) no longer a future perspective, (2) the desire to be dead although they were not seriously ill and (3) a persistent death wish. In the second section the research subject was the development of the wish to die in time.

4.3.2. Experiences in connection with the wish to die

The aim of the in-depth interviews was to deepen the results of the quantitative research, to make them clearer and more precise. The respondent's questions concerning their own life and its worth with all the doubts about it occurred primarily in the conversations that developed during the interviews.

A concrete active wish to die was generally less explicitly expressed. Several of the interviewees, although they seemed to have already been preparing their death, presently had no actual wish to end their life. That is not so surprising, as one can doubt, whether those who still are willing to participate in a survey as the "Perspective Research", are already so directly near to take the step to pass away. It is more probably that those who want to participate in such research still have doubts and the hope that they can find an alternative, perhaps a last resort in connection with the research.[83]

4.3.3. The development of the death-wish in time

The second section of the quantitative research existed of a longitudinal analysis of the 37 interviews that were taken at certain moments in 2013, 2017, and 2019 among a group of 18 persons. This analysis makes visible how the death wish of seniors can develop.

Between 2013 and 2017 some of the respondents ended their life. The conversations that took place before, were focussing on the event in positive and negative perspectives: On the one hand it was judged as a free, proactive choice, a kind of self-determination, a manner of controlling and bearing responsibility, and on the other hand as a doom, the only way to prevent a disaster. In 2017 there were also respondents, whose death wish had decreased in result of new

---

83 Els van Wijngaarden et al., p. 16.

social relations. Nevertheless, they ended their lives shortly after. In other cases, the wish to die increased and became persistent through the years. However, although they wanted to end their life, they were not able to commit suicide or did not dare to do it. Furthermore, there were people whose wish to die did diminish through the years. They found new perspectives and possibilities that let their will to live return. In one case, the wish to die diminished after the medicine to commit suicide was to the person's disposal. In some cases, the desire to die just vanished, sometimes only for a certain period, sometimes for good, for example, because new bindings with other people and/or with the whole society had developed.

The qualitative research among the seniors with a wish to die, not being seriously ill, completed the results of the quantitative research by adding various important details.

Els van Wijngaarden et al. were quite right, when they concluded that both qualitative studies together offer good insights into the ambivalence and dynamics in relation to wishes and desires concerning living and dying. There also exist fundamental differences between the different age-groups and even innumerable differences between individuals. That is completely natural and not new. But it leads to the question whether there is no further research with a more detailed questionnaire and a bigger number of respondents of all age groups necessary to get a better close-up of the existing problems and the differences between individuals and social groupings.

Overviewing the results of the "Perspective Research", one can summarize that they offer new actual empirical material about the life of people being 55 years of age and older, not being ill, with a wish to end life. This knowledge can be useful as a basis for new considerations and reflections in connection with the search for an adequate perspective for people with a death wish and the respective legal regulations. The lacking broad interdisciplinarity of this research, however, the missing of a focus on so important subjects as Dutch and European law, several psychological, psychiatric, and sociological aspects ask for additional studies and research. A more interdisciplinary study already was performed by the Royal Dutch Medical Association (KNMG)[84] for the smaller, but extra problematical subject "Euthanasia in Cases of Dementia".[85]

---

84 See below Part 2,6.
85 See below.

5. The judgement of the Supreme Court[86] of the Netherlands of April 21st, 2020[87]

5.1. Introduction and the facts of the case

It took many years before the Supreme Court of the Netherlands finally had to decide for the first time a case in which the Law on Euthanasia 2001 played the decisive role.

The facts of this case were as follows:

In 2016, a medical doctor, specialized in geriatric medicine, working in a nursing home in The Hague, carried out euthanasia on a 74-year-old woman, who suffered from Alzheimer's disease. After she had heard the respective diagnosis in 2012, she wrote down a euthanasia statement together with a dementia statement in which she explained that she wanted euthanasia in the case she was no longer able to live at her home. The reasons for this were the experiences she had when her mother was suffering from dementia and was forced to stay in a nursing home. She declared in her statement that she really did not want to live in a nursing home. In 2015, she made some changes in her euthanasia statement, that could be understood as restrictions, by using the words "when I, myself think that the time has come" and "on my request".

After the woman was brought to a nursing home, her husband asked the doctor to act in accordance with her euthanasia statement. The doctor did medical examinations and contacted two independent medical doctors who were convinced that all juridical conditions for euthanasia were fulfilled. The woman herself by then was totally incapable of performing legal acts and talked regularly very variably about her wish to die. After the woman had stayed in the nursing home for 8 weeks, the doctor decided to carry out euthanasia without before talking again with her about his decision. Firstly, he gave the woman a premedication, a sleeping draught, in her coffee. Despite this premedication, the woman came upright while the doctor injected the euthanatica and she had to be held on so long as the euthanatica were given.

The Regional Euthanasia Review Commission (RTE)[88] that examined the case in 2016 was convinced that the doctor had not acted in conformity with

---

86 Hoge Raad der Nederlanden.

87 ECLI: NL:HR: 2020:712.

88 RTE = Regionale Toetsingscommissie Euthanasie.
The "Euthanasia Code 2018" describes the issues the RTEs regards as relevant for the review of notifications of termination of life on request and assisted suicide (English,euthanasiecommissie.nl/code-of-practice).

art. 2 (1) sub a and f Law on Euthanasia and based this opinion primarily on the changes that were made in the euthanasia statement by the patient in 2015. The RTE suggested that the woman was convinced to be able to ask for euthanasia at a later moment. Furthermore, the RTE had doubts about the correctness of the premedication because it was given in secret and about the patient's reaction on the injection that possibly had to be interpreted as a sign of resistance.

The conclusion of the RTE was that the doctor did not act carefully, and it resulted in the fact that the case was sent through to the Board of Procurators General[89] and the Health Protection Inspectorate. Their examinations resulted in a writ of summons in the criminal court and a disciplinary complaint in the medical disciplinary tribunal.

The public prosecutor was convinced that in the face of the facts of the case, the doctor could not have been convinced that the wish of the woman was voluntary and deliberate. The doctor was obliged to ask the woman again in advance and to protect her, if necessary, against her own former declaration, dating from the time when she still was capable to perform legal acts, such as the changes in her euthanasia statement. Accordingly, the public prosecutor decided that not a privileged punishment ex art. 293,1 Dutch Criminal Code (intentionally ending the life of somebody else according to his/her express and serious desire), but art. 289 Dutch Criminal Code (murder with a maximum of lifelong prison sentence) was applicable.

The court in The Hague did not follow the public prosecutor but decided that the facts could not be defined as murder (art. 289 Dutch Criminal Code) but had to be interpreted as ending the woman's life according to her desire (art. 293,1 Dutch Criminal Code). The court stated that the doctor had exercised due care as the intense dementia of the woman made it impossible to talk with her about her actual sufferings and desires concerning life and death.

The Public Prosecutions Department did not agree with this judgement and therefore asked the Procurator General at the Supreme Court of the Netherlands to lodge a cassation in the interest of the law.

The Supreme Court stressed that there were no reasons to be found in the judgement of the court in The Hague to lodge a judgement in the interest of the law. Accordingly, the judgement of the court in The Hague that the doctor was not liable to punishment and had been discharged from further prosecution continued to exist.

---

89 College van Procureurs-Generaal.

5.2. The most important considerations of the Supreme Court and their grounds in the criminal case[90]

(1) Medical doctors are justified by art. 2 sub 2 Wtl[91] according to the history of the origin of this article - as the Supreme Court stated - to comply with the request to commit euthanasia, written while still being capable of performing legal acts, in cases patients meanwhile are suffering from even advanced dementia.

(2) The applicability of art. 2 sub 2 Wtl has the consequence that also the six duties of care of art. 2 sub 1 Wtl must be taken into consideration as far as possible correspondingly. The Supreme Court considered hereby, that under the special circumstances of advanced dementia these duties possibly also can need special interpretations in consequence of the fact that dementia can lead to extended dramatic alterations of the personality of individuals. The Supreme Court also stressed that in these 'special cases' the fulfilment of the duties of care also has to compensate the incapacity of the demented person to make up his/her will and to express it.

In the concrete case two duties of care are of special importance (1) The medical doctor must have got the persuasion that the request of the person in question was voluntary and well-considered (art. 2 sub 1 a) and (2) that the patient was suffering hopelessly and unbearably (art. 2 sub 1 b). A meticulous interpretation of the written request, not only of the words, but at the same time of all circumstances, is needed. According to the considerations of the Supreme Court it is important and decisive, that the medical doctor finds out what the patient wanted to declare in the written request. Hereby he/she also must consider possible contra indications. These contra indications can also occur after the patient no longer is able to form and to express a relevant will. The physical and psychical conditions of the patient can force a medical doctor to recognize that the patient's condition is not the one, the patient had thought of when writing the request.

(3) In contrast to the public prosecutor, the Supreme Court considered that the patient must not verify again his/her will to die shortly before euthanasia takes place if the patient in question is no longer able to express his/her

---

90 Hoge Raad, 21-4-2020, ECLI:NL: HR:2020:712, in short: 6. Summary & End.
91 Wtl (sometimes WTL) = **W**et **t**oetsing **l**evensbeëindiging op verzoek en hulp bij zelfdoding: Dutch Law on Euthanasia.

relevant will. In a case as the present, the medical doctor may base his/her action just on the patient's former written request.

(4) Furthermore, as already stated above, the medical doctor must have got the persuasion that the patient is suffering hopeless unbearably. In connection with this condition the Supreme Court declared that the legislator already took the possibility into account, that men who do not suffer from physical complaints, nevertheless, can suffer hopeless unbearably by their advanced dementia. However, the Supreme Court did not count the "unacceptable living conditions" of the patient as such as unbearable sufferings. The Supreme Court claimed that additionally there must exist special significant signs for unbearable suffering, which the medical doctor can recognize for example in the behaviour of the patient.

(5) The Supreme Court also stated that as far as it concerns medical doings, the carefulness must be judged primarily in accordance with the norms and insights of medical professionals. The judge should adopt an attitude of reserve so far. As medical actions underlie not only criminal – but also disciplinary law, the Supreme Court held the opinion that prosecution is not necessarily always the best solution. This opinion agrees with that of the Public Prosecution Department.[92]

(6) The Supreme Court also declared that euthanasia must take place under for the patient most comfortable circumstances. Accordingly, a medical doctor may use a premedication to sedate a patient in cases in which the situation makes this necessary, independently of the fact whether the patient was informed in advance or not.

(7) The Supreme Court concluded also (6.2) that the legislator took in consideration that in cases in which dementia plays a decisive role, always difficult weightings with generally not self-evident conclusions are coming up. Nevertheless, the legislator established even for persons suffering from advanced dementia the possibility to get relieved from unbearable sufferings and pain.

5.3. The judgement of the Supreme Court in the respective disciplinary case[93]

The Supreme Court set the decision of the Central Medical Disciplinary Tribunal

---

92 OM-Aanwijzing vervolgingsbeslissing in zake actieve levensbeëindiging op verzoek.
93 ECLI (European Case Law Identifier): NL: HR: 2020: 713, 21-04-2020.

(CTG)[94] of March 19th, 2019[95] aside. The administrative court was convinced that the medical doctor did not act in agreement with her duty of care based on art. 2 sub 1 a and f Wtl and imposed a reprimand. The Supreme Court stressed in his judgment of April 21st, 2020 (5.1-5.4), that it obviously is the task of the administrative court to take the opinion of the Regional Review Committee Euthanasia (RTE) into account; however, the administrative judge is not obliged just to follow the RTE's decisions but to investigate the case independently thoroughly and to decide further accordingly whether the medical doctor acted in the frame of the norms and standards of the medical profession.

In connection with the interpretation of the written request of the patient the Supreme Court considered in the same judgement (6.1-6.6) that this request must not be interpreted only verbatim but also with the help of circumstances that offer insights into the intentions the patient had. Therefore, the opinion of the Central Medical Disciplinary Tribunal that the request may not be interpreted is not true.

6. The Royal Dutch Medical Association[96] (KNMG) and the judgment of the Supreme Court of April 21st, 2020

The KNMG summarized the main considerations of the Supreme Court for its members to help them who are regularly confronted with difficult situations in connection with requests of euthanasia. Together with the Royal Dutch Association for the promotion of Pharmacy[97] (KNMP) the KNMG published **"Guidelines for the Practice of Euthanasia and Assisted Suicide" in 2012.**[98] The KNMP "Standards for Euthanasia" 2007 were their point of departure. The Guidelines are regularly updated. They have the task to make sure that Euthanasia and assisted suicide are practiced effectively and safely. To the content belong: The choice of medication and dosage, the description of the procedure for the medical doctors and the required resources, the description of criteria of due care for pharmacists, the recording of help desk and vade mecum for medical doctors and pharmacists, the agreements regarding possible future adjustments of the guidelines based on the aforementioned evaluations or other

94 Centraal Tuchtcollege Gezondheidszorg (CTG)
95 ECLI: NL: TGZCTG: 2019:68, Centraal Tuchtcollege voor de Gezondheidszorg, Den Haag c 2018:352.
96 Koninklijke Nederlandse Maatschappij ter bevordering der Pharmacie.
97 Royal Dutch Pharmacists Association.
98 KNMG/KNMP, Guidelines 2012: www.Knmg.nl/english

developments and recommendations for promoting the distribution and application of the guidelines.[99]

In the summary of the judgement of the Supreme Court of the **21st of April 2020** the KNMG reported that this judgement does not solve special dilemmas that exist for medical doctors in connection with euthanasia in cases of (advanced) dementia. The relatively wide decision-making freedom the Supreme Court offered the medical doctors can also cause extra difficulties: Family members of patients exert pressure on doctors by arguing "the judge decided that euthanasia in cases of (advanced) dementia is permissible". Medical doctors regularly feel this pressure as very heavy. In connection with the judgement of the Supreme Court of the 21st of April 2020, the KNMG therefore stated again unambiguously that this judgement did not change the law: euthanasia still is not a right, and medical doctors are not obliged to conduct euthanasia.

In **August 2020,** the KNMG was busy with the project "Euthanasia in Cases of Dementia" to help the medical doctors to find adequate decisions in these difficult situations. Quantitative and qualitative research took place. Experts in the fields of ethics, law, and social sciences as well as the KNMG panel members were interviewed about euthanasia in cases of dementia. In this way important information could be collected that was handed to focus-groups of medical doctors experienced with these cases of euthanasia. In these groups the focus was directed to the process of decision making in respective cases, especially on problems medical doctors experience regularly in connection with the requirements of due care. In the frame of the project "Euthanasia in Cases of Dementia" there were also interviews taken with volunteer help organisations. Furthermore, the relevant literature and the jurisprudence in respective cases were studied. All knowledge collected, then was involved in the development of a concept-vision, which was tested by internet consultation by medical doctors and in society. Then, a publication on euthanasia in cases of dementia was prepared by the KNMG together with the KNMP and published on the 1st of December 2021[100] as a special chapter of the latest version of the guideline on the implementation of euthanasia and assisted suicide.

---

99 KNMG/KNMP, Guidelines for the Practice of Euthanasia and Physician Assisted Suicide, 5th edition, 2012, p. 8.

100 Richtlijn Uitvoering euthanasie en hulp bij zelfdoding, KNMG en KNMP, September 2021; www. knmg.nl./advies-richtlijnen/dossiers/euthanasie.htm. See below Part 2, 9.3.

7. The introduction of the "Completed Life" draft-bill in parliament

On **July 17th, 2020,** the Left Liberals (D'66)[101] presented their bill on "Completed Life" in parliament. This bill proposes the introduction of a law that offers a possibility for seniors aged 75 years and older, **not being ill,** to end their life. The 75 years border was chosen because people of this age had already had a relatively long life. The proposed regulation is thought of as a supplement to the Law on Euthanasia. During the coalition of Rutte III an acceptance of this bill was very improbable. Meanwhile, the next Dutch General Election for the House of Representatives took place on the 17th of March 2021, in which 37 political parties participated. The result as such makes the forming of a coalition not easier than in 2017. While the right-wing liberals only got one seat more (now 34 seats), the right-wing populists won 6 seats (now 8 seats) and the left-wing liberals (D' 66) 5 seats (now 24 seats), the green lefts lost 6 seats (now 8 seats), the socialist party lost 5 (now 9 seats), and the Christian Democratic Appel 4 seats (now 15 seats). The right-wing Party of Freedom lost 3 seats and now has 17 seats. The Labour Party got 9 seats as in 2017. Only on the 10th January 2022, the new government Ruttw IV was sworn in. The new Minister of Health is medical doctor Ernst Kuipers (D' 66).

Before the initiator of the bill on "Completed Life", Member of Parliament Pia Dijkstra (D' 66) introduced her proposal on the 17th of July 2020,[102] she had the possibility to read and recognize the results of the "Perspective Research"[103] that was focussing on people with a death wish aged 55 years and more and was published in January 2020. A result of her cognizance of this research was that she adopted into her bill (under the condition that the person who declared "to be ready with life" had agreed) the integration of family and family doctors into the euthanasia route as a means that could strengthen the probability that the decision to end the completed life was well considered and not caused by pressure of others. Another important result of the "Perspective Research" was the fact, that among the 20,000 interviewed people not being seriously ill aged 55 years and older, not more than 0.03% declared that during the last week their wish to die was stronger than their wish to live. This finding makes the need of the

---

101 P. van den Dool, NRC/Handelsblad, 18-07-2020, p. 8.
102 Wetsvoorstel 35534-2.
103 Els van Wijngaarden et al., 2020.

introduction of a special legal regulation for so relatively few people question-able for some.[104] However, was the underlying question the interviewees had to answer really the right one to get the answer the interviewers were looking for? A parliamentary debate about the bill will take place in the new parliament.

8. Euthanasia and palliative sedation[105]

As well as euthanasia there are several actions in the medical domain used to end, or at least reduce, unbearable suffering when the end of life is near and when there is no realistic chance of getting better: namely palliative sedation[106], ending medical treatment, stopping supply of food, drink and moisture, intensi-fication of pain reduction by sedatives and refraining from resuscitation.[107]

The different effects of all these are difficult to establish as they are often used one after the other, or together, and they regularly interact.

Of importance, however, is to be always aware of the main differences be-tween euthanasia and all the other means in the medical domain[108]:

1) The aim of euthanasia is to end life, the patient dies in consequence of euthanasia - a planned intervention. The aim of palliative sedation, however, is to take away as far as possible pain and suffering by reducing consciousness as far as is necessary. It is not the aim of palliative sedation to shorten life and in the case where it is practised according to KNMG guidelines, it generally does not shorten life[109] and the patient finally dies in consequence of the illness he or she had.

However, in 2018 of the 35,000 cases of palliative sedation that took place in the Netherlands, 90% of the patients died after a few days, while only 5% lived

---

104 Govert den Hartogh, Pia Dijkstra's voltooid-leven wet is onnodig, NRC/Handelsblad. 03-08-2020, p. E 18-E 19.
105 Palliative sedation is regularly talked about in hospital and by doctors as "comfort treatment".
106 W. Distelmans, Palliatieve Sedatie, Trage Euthanasie of Sociale Dood, Houtekiet, Ant-werpen 2017; G.A. ten Hartogh, Palliatieve sedatie en euthanasie. Commentaar op een richtlijn, Tijdschrift voor Gezondheidsrecht 2006, 30 (2), 90-96.
107 https://www.pallialine.nl/index.php?pagina=/richtline/item/pagina.php&id=28948&richtlijn_id=632; L. van Zuylen et al., De dokter en de dood. Opti-male zorg in de laatste levensfase, Bohn Stafleu van Loghum, Houten 2018.
108 www.nu.nl>gezondheids>wat-is-het-verschil-tussen (09-12-2020), 20-02-2022
109 Knmg.nl/advies-richtlijnen/dossiers/paliatieve-zorg-en-palliatieve-sedatie.htm per 29 -11-2021.

longer than one week. According to cardiologist Dijkgraaf,[110] the reason for the fact that most patients die so quickly after palliative sedation has started is that palliative sedation is mostly combined with reducing, or stopping, medicine, nutrition and hydration. Furthermore, sedatives can reduce breathing. Shortening life has the positive effect of reducing suffering, but it may not be the result of palliative sedation. Shortening life belongs to euthanasia and for euthanasia there exist very special legal regulations. In practice, however, medical doctors usually prefer and therefore tend to act in the frame of their medical domain, "deliberately using vague communication" when talking about the so-called "comfort treatment with their patients" to be able to avoid official reporting, possible legal consequences and also probable emotional loads for themselves.[111] Accordingly, one can suppose that palliative sedation might be relatively often used in cases that actually belong to the category of euthanasia.

2) Euthanasia must be based on a request of the patient, while palliative sedation is a medical doctor's decision taken when he/she is convinced that the patient will not recover. According to the respective guideline of the KNMG, palliative sedation is limited to use in cases in which the life expectancy of the patient is not more than two weeks. Even laymen will be able to understand the difficulty of a right calculation in these cases. For this estimation, much will depend on the individual doctor, his or her personality, general view of life, life experience, medical training and so on, but also on the individual patient and his or her general health situation, of which the respective doctor often will not be sufficiently informed. Accordingly, there just exist "large margins"[112] in connection with the calculations of the time a patient still has to live.

In cases of palliative sedation, it is very important that the doctor chooses the right time to start and that he informs the patient properly. Both requirements are, in practice, often not properly carried out.

3) The procedure of euthanasia is regulated precisely. Euthanasia can be planned, even far in advance, however palliative sedation, belongs to general medical practice with its own special regulations. To plan palliative sedation is generally not possible.

Guidelines of the Royal Dutch Medical Association (KNMG) for palliative sedation have existed since 2005. In 2008 a questionnaire was sent to 1,580 medical

---

110 R. Dijkgraaf, Volkskrant of 16 - 02 - 2022, Opinie: Goed dat praten over levenseinde wordt aangemoedigd, maar leg uit dat er verschillende soorten hulp bij doodgaan zijn.
111 R. Dijkgraaf, Volkskrant of 16-02-2022.
112 R. Dijkgraaf, Volkskrant of 16 - 02 -2022, Opinion.

doctors with questions about the last patient they treated with "comfort" (continuous palliative sedation). Only 36% of the addressees answered. Shortness of breath, pain and physical exhaustion were the main reasons for the treatment. In 18% of the cases the only reason was empathy. Life expectancy of 97% of the patients was less than 2 weeks. In 81% of the cases the medical doctors were present when the palliative sedation started. In 92% of the cases midazolam was used and 41% of the medical doctors agreed that the sedation had a certain life-shortening effect. Most of them declared that the suffering of the patient was reduced, a "good quality of dying was reached" and that the family was satisfied. In most cases the palliative sedation took place in accordance with the guidelines of the KNMG. Finally, the medical doctors stated that, in their opinion, more special attention should be paid to the difficulties they had in starting the palliative sedation and to the possibility of the existence of life-shortening effects.

In 2009 the guidelines of the KNMG were amended. At present, (2022), a new version is being prepared. Medical doctors who are looking for information and help in connection with palliative sedation can contact the respective consulting teams of the KNMG.

There still, (2022), exists relatively much uncertainty concerning the medical practice in connection with palliative sedation and accordingly also doubts and insecurity amongst the public and amongst medical doctors. The doubts people, mainly medical doctors, have in relation to palliative sedation and euthanasia were strengthened by the following lawsuit[113]:

In 2013, Nico Trump, a family doctor, decided to practice, notwithstanding the respective guidelines, palliative sedation in a case of an obviously terminal patient who suffered unbearably from cancer. His co-assistant informed the responsible health care authorities of the fact that the doctor gave a too-high dose of morphine. There was no hearing. Doctor Trump was charged with murder and this was made public. Shortly after, the accused committed suicide.

Was what happened really a penal law case? Had the case not better been decided by a disciplinary committee? A commission of inquiry was formed. In 2015 this commission presented its report and in 2016 the Council of State declared the charge against Nico Trump unlawful.

According to the Dutch Christian Organisation, "Care for Life", an opponent of euthanasia, medical doctors use palliative sedation, also "improper", as a "euthanasia light" to shorten life. The Voluntary Euthanasia Association[114] (NVVE),

---

113 NOS, nieuwsuur of 03-05-2019, 21:29
114 Nederlandse Vereniging voor Vrijwillige Euthanasie (NVVE).

in favour of euthanasia, considers palliative sedation suitable as legitimate alternative for euthanasia as long as the patient and the family are informed and both agree. The KNMG stated that medical doctors mostly do not use palliative sedation as means to bypass their existing guidelines.[115]

An important reason for the present broad discussion about palliative sedation in public, and in politics, is the fact that the numbers of palliative sedation cases has risen rather quickly during recent years, something that worries the government, but also the Voluntary Euthanasia Association[116]. Therefore, they have both proposed scientific research to find out the reasons for this development.

While in 2005, 8.2% of the people who died were treated with palliative sedation before their death, in 2015 this was already 18.3% and at present (2022) almost 25% is estimated.[117] The questions one is interested in are, among others, whether the fact that at present more people are cared for at home and in nursing homes is a reason for this growth, whether the relatively new wish of people to have direct control over their end of life is influential and what the statistics of palliative sedation in relation to those of euthanasia are like. Respondents are medical doctors, relatives of the patients and scientists. The result of this research is not yet known.

9. Euthanasia and demented people

9.1. Critical comments of the Health and Youth Inspection and the Medical Disciplinary Board

Not so long ago[118], the Dutch Public Health and Youth Inspection[119], a government body and part of the Ministry of Health, that supervises the quality of the care sector, medical products and the youth assistance as well as the rights of patients and clients and the Medical Disciplinary Tribunals[120], whose task it is to

---

115 M. v. d. Wier, Trouw of 25-06-2019.

116 M. v. d. Wier, Trouw of 25-06-2019.

117 NOS 14-06-2019.

118 F.Weeda, NRC/Handelsblad, 19-08-2020.

119 Inspectie voor de Gezondheidszorg, https://www.Igj.nl

120 Medisch Tuchtcollege. There exist 5 Regional Tribunals and one Central Medical Tribunal. They work on basis of the Individual Health Care Professionals Act/Medical Code of Practice. There exist plans to reorganize the Dutch Medical Code of Practice, see: Bill of 31-08-2020 for a modification of the Law on the professions in the individual health care in connection with the organisation of the Regional Medical Disciplinary Tribunals, Parliamentary Documents II 2019/20, 35547, nr. 1- 4.

control the quality of the professional practice of the professionals of individual health care were criticised again in the practice of euthanasia in cases of dementia.[121] Members of tribunals are legal and medical professionals. They have the task to control whether and in how far the professionals of the individual health care meet the requirements their profession claims. The means the Medical Disciplinary Tribunals have to their proposal are warnings, fines, and the temporary or permanent prohibition of pursuing one's profession.

In the case concerned, a medical doctor, specialized in gerontology and working at the Expert Centre Euthanasia[122], the former End of Life Clinic[123], got a warning from a Medical Disciplinary Tribunal[124], because she had not sufficiently reasoned why she did not follow up the advice of the "SCEN-doctor"[125]. According to the opinion of this specially trained medical doctor who has the task to offer support and compulsory advice to doctors who are involved in realizing euthanasia, the geriatrist's decision to consent in the case in question was wrong. The euthanasia took place in 2017 based on a respective written declaration of the patient dating from 2011 in which she had declared that she would not want to live any longer under the condition that she had to suffer mentally unbearably and had to be placed in a nursing home. The geriatrist studied the SCEN doctor's advice thoroughly and discussed it in a multidisciplinary consultation with six experienced medical doctors and nurses, who all shared her opinion that the advice of the SCEN doctor was not convincing. In consequence she decided to deviate from the SCEN doctor's advice and gave her respective reasons. According to the opinion of Steven Pleiter, managing director of the Expert Centre Euthanasia[126], the former End of Life Clinic, euthanasia after a negative advice of SCEN doctors is principally possible as the law does not strictly require a positive advice.[127] The Medical Disciplinary Tribunal[128], however, held the opinion that the geriatrist in the concrete case, before performing euthanasia had the duty

---

121 F. Weeda, NRC/Handelsblad, 19-08-2020.

122 Expertise Centrum Euthanasie.

123 Levenseindekliniek.

124 Tuchtrechter.

125 Steun en Consultatie bij Euthanasie in Nederland.

126 Expertisecentrum Euthanasie.

127 Steven Pleiter, in: Frederiek Weeda, "Inspectie weer kritisch over euthanasie bij dementie", NRC/Handelsblad, 19-08-2020.

128 RTG (Regionaal Tuchtcollege Gezondheidszorg) Amsterdam, 17-08-2020/064 ECLI: NL: TGZRAMS 2020:93.

to report to the SCEN doctor that she could not accept his advice and to ask him to adapt the text or she had to consult another independent SCEN doctor. Here the question rises whether the procedure about the cooperation of the SCEN doctors and the practitioners who must execute euthanasia is regulated so clearly that the geriatrist was informed enough about the need to contact the SCEN doctor in question about his advice or to ask another SCEN doctor for a second opinion. If not, she nevertheless should have tried to take this step. Her lack of duty in this case would have been less serious. In the view of the importance of the interest protected by law utmost care must be performed anyhow, but not only by the practitioner, but also by the SCEN doctors and their relevant supervising instances. The introduction of an instance as that of SCEN doctors makes only sense if these doctors have the means to realise their tasks. Important in this respect is that their advice count. Furthermore, the critic of the Medical Disciplinary Tribunal and the SCEN doctor was focussing on the same facts, namely that the geriatrist did not explain sufficiently why the patient's suffering were unbearable and why she did not try to solve these sufferings with adequate alternative means.

9.2. The proposal to make euthanasia for demented elderly people possible already in an earlier state

Euthanasia in cases of dementia can be assessed as the problem most difficult to solve of all problems concerning euthanasia. On occasion of the above[129] described case and the lack of clarity concerning the due caution that must be considered, Klaas Rozemond proposed[130] that the Medical Disciplinary Tribunals should explain the existing duty of care more explicitly. He stressed that the present indistinctness is caused for a great deal by the possibility to perform euthanasia on demented people based on declarations of intention, written even long ago.[131] The requirements of due care in these cases are not described in sufficient detail in the Dutch Law on Euthanasia and the written

---

129 Part 2, 9. 1.
130 Klaas Rozemond, Associate Professor Department of Criminal Law, Free University of Amsterdam, Euthanasie demente ouderen kan beter in vroeg stadium NRC/Handelsblad, 01-09-2020, p. 18. Recently, Rozemond wrote a book on "The self-chosen end of life", ISVW NL Uitgevers, ISBN 978-90-831 21-58-1.
131 In April 2021 Liselotte Postma obtained her doctorate with a thesis on: Regulation of the written declaration euthanasia in article 2 sub 2 Euthanasia Law from Criminal Law perspective.

declarations in these cases often are not unambiguous. Regularly demented people are no longer able to form and/or express their will concerning euthanasia and to describe their unbearable sufferings clearly. According to Rozemond the consequence of these circumstances is that medical doctors must interpret where clarity is missing. The extent of these interpretations by individual medical doctors causes much arbitrariness. The consequence according to Rozemond is, that "it depends on the respective medical doctor, whether euthanasia is well or not permitted". To prevent this undesirable situation, he proposed to permit euthanasia already in an earlier stadium, namely when patients are still able to decide and explain their will themselves and he ended with the conclusion that medical practitioners should be able to answer questions for help in connection with euthanasia simply saying: "I help you, when you want it".

The proposal of Rozemond is theoretically clear and correct, the question however is, whether it can be used as a working basis in practice. This question can be answered only by medical specialists. There exist many gradations between a sound mind and dementia in the end stadium with changes in the course of time and great variations between the individuals. Is it possible to develop and lay down a clear definition for the borderline between being able and being no longer able to form a will and to explain it?

According to Barry Reisberg of New York University, School of Medicine's Silberstein Aging and Dementia Research Centre,[132] for example, there are 7 stages[133] to distinguish: Stage 1: no impairment; stage 2: Very mild decline; stage 3: Mild cognitive problems that physicians are able to detect, people in this stage have problems to find the right words in conversations, to make plans and to organize, to remember names and they often loose personal possessions; this stage is lasting about 7 years; stage 4: Moderate decline, clearcut symptoms of the disease, people have difficulties with easy arithmetic, a poor short-time memory, are no longer able to pay bills, forget details of their life history; the duration of this stage is estimated to last 2 years; in stage 5 follows a moderately severe decline, people now need help in every-day life activities; this phase is lasting about 1 1/2 years; stage 6: The decline is severe, patients now need constant supervision and often professional care, major personality changes and various behaviour problems appear; this stage is lasting generally about 2 ½ years; stage 7: The decline is very severe now,

---

132 Functional Assessment Staging (FAST), 1988.
133 https://www.alzheimers.net/stages-of-alzheimers-disease.

people lose the ability to communicate and to respond to their environment. They have no insight in their condition and need help with everything; this terminal phase can last for 5 years and more.

At least before the background of a general scheme as that of Barry Reisberg in which individual specialities still are not at all considered, the question about the content of a regulation for the right time to ask a physician for help to commit euthanasia should be answered.

9.3. The chapter on demented people in the KNMG and KNMP guideline "Implementation of Euthanasia and Assisted Suicide" 2021

The updated guideline has the task to support medical doctors to find the right decision to provide care at the end of life. An important new part of the guideline is the chapter regarding euthanasia in cases of demented people. The aim of this chapter is to give medical doctors something to hold on, in order to find solutions for these difficult situations together with their patients and the patients' families.

In this chapter, the fact is stressed that a written euthanasia statement of a patient is not more than the beginning of a conversation with the medical doctor, not at all its end.

Generally, euthanasia in cases of advanced dementia is only possible if a written euthanasia statement exists that was written while the patient was still capable to perform juridic acts. Medical doctors always should have the possibility to discuss the whole situation with the patient and the patient's family. In cases patients are no longer able to give informed consent, medical doctors should nevertheless try to communicate with them. In any case, it is necessary to judge the patient's suffering thoroughly and to think about alternatives.

For many medical doctors, euthanasia in cases of patients who are no longer able to declare their own will committing euthanasia is unacceptable. Therefore, the guideline stresses that it is important to talk with the doctor on time, so that the patient can declare his will clearly and the doctor has the possibility to give the patient his/her vision respectively his/her limits. Every medical doctor should have the possibility to make his own considerations. Also. in cases the legal regulation offers the possibility for committing euthanasia the individual doctor is not obliged to end a life. However, the KNMG also stated that it considers it of importance to support those medical doctors who are willing to commit euthanasia in complex situations.

According to the guideline, there is only limited room for the interpretation of the written euthanasia statements. Next to the family, the consultation of experts and involved caregivers can be helpful. Regularly, family members can be an important source of information, but they should not be motivated to give rise of decisions about the end of life, that can have dreadful consequences for the auctor himself.

The guideline also stresses that the medical doctor should talk with the patient about premedication and that all results of the conversation should be registered and motivated.

Basis for most of the points of view of the guideline was the above discussed judgement of the Supreme Court of the Netherlands of the 21st of April 2020.

10. Free access to lethal means?

Almost at the end of the preparation of this treatise on euthanasia in the Netherlands, Govert den Hartogh's article appeared in the Netherlands Law Journal in which he discussed the question whether free access to lethal remedies should be allowed.[134]

The author, professor emeritus of Ethics at Amsterdam University and from 1998–2010 member of the Regional Review Commission Euthanasia stresses in his introduction the fact, that most Dutch people are not content with the present legal regulation of euthanasia and assisted suicide, because, according to their opinion, the law is too restricted. Mainly people are not content with the extent of due care that is demanded but also with the fact that lethal means are next to not available. Mainly people with so-called complex problems, such as psychiatric disturbances, several geriatric problems at the same time, the beginning of dementia and people who according to the opinion of others are not really suffering unbearably, all being ill, but not necessarily near death, are examples for this group of patients. In this connection Den Hartogh cited the fact that in 2018 30% of the requests the Expert Centre Euthanasia received, were rejected as not being in accordance with the standards of due care.[135]

Another group of people want to have guaranteed access to lethal means apart from requirements of due care just for the case they later might need them.

---

134 Nederlands Juristenblad (NJB) 2020, nr. 29, p. 2136–2142.
135 G. den Hartogh, NJB 2020, p. 2137.

The centre of Den Hartogh's article on access to lethal means is the question whether sufficiently effective safety means can be developed to prevent abuse of a regulation on free access to lethal remedies. This subject is the crux of the problem of euthanasia which until now was hardly any time before really discussed in the Netherlands.

As starting point for his explanations Den Hartogh chose the statement, that the Right to respect for private and family life in Article 8 European Convention of Human Rights[136] could be the most principal argument for the right of access to lethal means.[137] Notable for so far is that Den Hartogh did not choose so far a Dutch, but an European legal regulation. The reason might be that in the First Part of the Dutch Constitution where the Dutch Fundamental Rights are summarized, the respective formulated right to inviolability of one's body[138] is worked out in details even less than the also as open-ended characterized[139] Art. 8 ECHR.

In his respective article, Den Hartogh did not discuss in how far the Dutch Constitution and perhaps other regulations than Art. 8 of the ECHR can form a fundamental basis for free access to lethal means, but concentrated straight away on Art. 8 ECHR, the article on which the European Court of Human Rights already decided in several cases since 2011, that man has the right "to

---

136 Art. 8 ECHR:
  (1) Everybody has the right to respect for his private and family life, his home and his correspondence.
  (2) There shall be no interference by a public authority with the exercise of his right except such as is in accordance with the law and is necessary in a democratic society in the interests of national security, public safety, or the economic well-being of the country, for the prevention of disorder or crime, for the protection of health or morals, or for the protection of the rights and freedoms of others.
137 Den Hartogh, NJB 2020, p. 2136 and following, p. 2137.
138 Art. 11 Dutch Constitution as translated into English by the Dutch Ministry of the Interior and Kingdom Relations 2002 (www.minbzk.nl): Everybody shall have the right to inviolability of his person, without prejudice to restrictions laid down by or pursuant to Act of Parliament. In the Dutch version, one does not read the inviolability of his "person" but of his "lichaam" i./e. in English "body".
  B. C. v. Beers, ed. 2013, www.nederlandsrechtsstaat.nl/module/nlrs/script/viewer. asp?soort=commentaar&artike=11
139 E. Wicks, B. Rainey, C. Ovey (2014) The ECHR, ISBN 978-0-19-965508-3.

determine the manner and time of his own death",[140] a statement that in the view of Den Hartogh, who in his explanations also referred to the right of self-determination,[141] obviously includes a right to suicide.

If one believes that a right to suicide exists, one should also offer the opportunity to get access to lethal means that lead to a humane end. However, as the main task of the government is the protection of life, the access to lethal means cannot generally be free for everybody. The general prohibition can only be discontinued in cases in which individuals decided to end their life in agreement with their free will after thoroughly well-considering everything and long-lasting. As the ECHR stressed, it is necessary that these preconditions are regularly verified by authorities, because the right to suicide of a subject is only an exception to the general obligation of the state to protect life. Accordingly, it is necessary to look for a clear, sufficiently effective legal regulation, that makes sure that abuse of lethal means can be as far as possible excluded.

In this connection Den Hartogh discussed mainly two possibilities:

(1) Alteration of the Dutch Narcotic Act (Opium Act)
As first possibility Den Hartogh thought of a regulation that enables physicians to write prescriptions for barbiturates for patients who want to end their life in accordance with their free will, after due consideration and long-lasting conviction without the consequence that these prescriptions would be assessed as assisting in committing suicide.
In the following, Den Hartogh summarizes the risks a respective regulation might have for the about one million inhabitants in the Netherlands[142] whose lives are depending mainly on voluntary aid, people, who for about 50% are swamped with work, but also for inhabitants with psychological disorders for whom the temptation to take lethal means gets much stronger after a respective alteration of the Dutch Narcotics Act.[143]

(2) Removing Article 294 sub 2 Dutch Criminal Code

---

140 Den Hartogh, NJB 2020 p. 2139 citing EHRM, 20-01-2011, 31322/07(Haas/ Swiss); further EHRM 19-07- 2012, 497/09 (Koch/Germany); EHRM 14-05-2013, 67810/10 (Gross/ Swiss); EHRM 23-06-2015, 2078/15 (Nicklinson and Lamb/UK).

141 See Part 3.

142 Den Hartogh, NJB 2020, p. 2140.

143 Den Hartogh, NJB 2020, p. 2140.

Art. 294 sub 2 Dutch Criminal Code[144] declares assisting in suicide and providing with the means to commit suicide as principally punishable. There is not much difference between the two alternatives, but medical doctors mostly prefer assistance in suicide in which the will of the patient is more prominently present than in the case of euthanasia.[145] Patients, however, often give preference to euthanasia because they have problems to kill themselves. This empirical fact allows the assumption that free access to lethal means itself would not necessarily lead to an increased demand.[146]

In his conclusion Den Hartogh summarizes, that art. 8 ECHR principally offers everybody who after due considering, freely and long-lasting decided to end his life the right to get lethal means, but that this right finds its limits, where the right on life of others must be protected. This need to protect third persons, mainly those who are not able to protect themselves, anyhow is to a certain extent, but not in any case, a matter of course. Decisive should be for so far, the answer to the question, whether and in how far there are not also other effective means to safeguard the security of these third persons than those that force people who want to take their own life to choose between staying in a subjectively experienced unbearable life or to die a horrible death for themselves, the persons with whom they are on close terms and often also third persons by suicide. Was this question already subject of research? Can the respective interests of the respective two groups be balanced? And if so, what are the results of this balancing and its consequences? Nobody, who did not decide to end the own life freely, may be forced or otherwise stimulated and initiated to do that. In general, it is not unconceivable that rights certain persons or groups of persons possess can cause certain dangers for others unintentionally, but that does not have the consequence that these rights must end, but that the negative consequences must be prevented. The easiness with which one blocks the possibility for people to end their life in a humane way by referring so generally to the need of protection of

---

144 Any person who intentionally assists in the suicide of a person or provides him with the means thereto shall, if suicide follows, be liable to a term of imprisonment not exceeding three years or a fine of the fourth category. Section 293 (2) shall apply mutatis mutandis.
  Art. 283 (2) says that medical doctors are not punishable if they meet the requirements of due care referred to in section 2 of the Termination of Life on Request and Assisted Suicide Act.

145 Den Hartogh, NJB 2020, p. 2140 and the cited literature.
146 Den Hartogh, NJB 2020. p. 2141, 29.

others, leads to the question whether this opinion is not inspired at least partly and perhaps even unconsciously, by the conviction that there cannot be, what "not may" be. Certainly, it is difficult to leave something behind that for century belonged to the main culture of the majority and that is not only rational present but also deeply internalized and felt.

Since old times, life is strongly protected by law. The present Dutch Constitution and several other legal regulations in force today, safeguard human life, while no law exists that deals with a right to take one's own life. In accordance with nature, human thinking and feeling, life is the absolute, superior fundamental right. Taking this into account, one must agree with Den Hartogh who declared it "not unthinkable" that the possibility to choose for those who wish to die, cannot be proved without testing their "self-assessment" concerning the existence of unbearable and hopeless sufferings[147] by experienced medical doctors, primarily psychiatrists. Furthermore, Den Hartogh proposed to look for more clarity concerning the limits of the medical domain[148] and to improve the knowledge about the possibilities, not eating and not drinking can offer as a "humane alternative"[149] to end life.

Voluntarily stopping or refusing eating and drinking, however, is not an easy alternative to end life. Depending on the general constitution of the individual person it can last up to some weeks. Those, who decide to choose this method to end their life without being acquainted enough with its circumstances, run the risk of very unpleasant or even dreadful experiences for themselves and those who offered their aid. Especially, voluntarily stopping or refusing eating and drinking should not be recommended to people who are not of age as for them, having to go and stay thirsty can be extremely hard to stand.[150] Generally one must state that voluntarily stopping eating and drinking is a method that is slowly and troublesome. There are surely people who want and are psychically able to end their life with such new last experiences, but many will not be mentally strong enough to go through this phase of slowly dying away without great troubles. Therefore, anyhow one should not inspire or even force others to choose this kind of death.[151] Even in connection with dying accompanied and

---

147 Den Hartogh, NJB 2020, p. 2141.
148 Den Hartogh, NJB 2020, p. 2141.
149 Den Hartogh, NJB 2020, p. 2142.
150 Ch. Walther, Sterbefasten - Chancen und Grenzen, Zeitschrift der Schweizerischen Gesellschaft für Palliative Medizin, Pflege und Begleitung, „palliative-ch" 2015 (3), p. 18–21.
151 Ch. Walther, palliative ch 2015 (3) 18-21.

supervised by medical doctors in hospital, stopping of eating and drinking seems to be difficult to practice so precisely, that states of panic, heavy hallucinations and other negative consequences are totally prevented.

For what concerns the demanded condition related to euthanasia that the wish to end life must be long-lasting, the minimum of two months chosen in the concept bill by Pia Dijkstra[152] and the proposal to stop or refuse eating and drinking voluntarily do not particularly agree with what the words "long lasting" describe. The addressees of these proposals only can be people whose end of life is already near-by and not all the people who want to safeguard that their death will be "good" sometime in future. There are many people who write a patient directive respectively a declaration of intention long in advance before they **want to die**. To make sure that their will expressed when writing did not change in later years, a legal regulation is needed that foresees in regular confirmations respectively updates of the former statement.

Den Hartogh finishes with the statement that one can expect from people who want to end their life that they accept that their respective decision is overviewed and judged by experienced physicians as the best way with which the state can protect as well the right to decide on one's own life as the right on the life of others.[153] However, getting acquainted with practice, results in the conclusion that one should not leave the patient and his or her family alone with the medical doctor to decide about the end of life. Every profession and specialism has a necessarily determined and restricted view. Medical doctors generally only know little of the personality of their patients and often they are not even well informed about the all over health condition of the patients during the last years. Therefore, a multidisciplinary staff should be permanent available so that in every concrete case the best possible know-how and help can be offered when decisions about the end of life are about to be taken. This is even more important in all the cases in which the medical doctors did not talk at all, not in time or not sufficiently with the patient and the respective family and the patient's consciousness is meanwhile due to illness and/or medication already reduced, as in these cases the family, too, is missing the information needed to decide correctly in the patient's interest. Furthermore and of greater importance: what rests of the individual Right of Self-Determination, if it depends on a review and judgement of medical doctors to whom the state has delegated a part of its responsibility to its subjects.

---

152 Concept of 18-12-2016.
153 Den Hartogh, NJB 2020, p. 2142.

11. Euthanasia and children beyond human aid, aged 1–12 years

Until now[154] active euthanasia can take place only in cases that babies up to one year and children of 12 years and older are suffering hopelessly and unbearable. For babies there exists a ministerial regulation with a precise guideline.[155] The respective conditions the medical profession developed are summarized in the so-called "Groninger Protocol".[156] Conditions in these cases also are hopeless and unbearable suffering and additionally the consent of the parents.

Children aged 12 years and older have the status of capable persons and therefore are under the Law on Euthanasia. Children from 12 to 16 years of age may ask for euthanasia themselves if their parents are informed, involved in the decision making and consent with the ending of life.

For incapable patients of 12 years and older legitimate euthanasia is not possible.

For children between the age of one and 12 years a special legal regulation is missing.[157] For them euthanasia is prohibited because they are unable to give informed consent. As far as there do not exist circumstances beyond one's control in a state of emergency caused by a conflict of duties[158], pain control and letting them die[159] are the general possibilities to reduce and end the sufferings of these children.

Ending life by stopping treatments that can lengthen life and/or stopping to give food and drinks are allowed for all age categories "in compliance with the legal regulations for medical and medical-professional standards".[160] In cases

---

154 October 2020.

155 Late Zwangerschapsafbreking en Actieve Levensbeëindiging Pasgeborenen (LZA/LP). https://wetten. overheid.nl/BWBR0037570/2018-08-01.

156 E. Verhagen, Pieter J. J. Sauer, The Groningen protocol - euthanasia in severely ill new-borns, New England Journal of Medicine 352.10 (2005) 959-962.

157 A.-M. van der Kaaden, Voor kind dat uitzichtloos lijdt, is er nog geen uitweg, NRC/ Handelsblad, 15-10- 2020, Binnenland, p. 9.

158 So far as known, there seems no respective case to be published in which this legal defence was used. M. Brouwer et al., Medische Beslissingen rond het Levenseinde bij Kinderen (1-12).

159 Laten versterven.

160 M. Brouwer et al., Medische Beslissingen rond het Levenseinde bij Kinderen (1-12), 28-09-2019, 1 b. Juridische context.

these means are chosen for, the process of dying can last rather long, up to about several weeks, an extremely traumatic event for parents, family, and friends.

According to the guideline of the Royal Dutch Society for the Promotion of Medicine palliative sedation is allowed if the patient suffers severely and his or her life expectancy is the most about two weeks.[161]

In October 2020, the Dutch Council of Ministers was confronted with the question whether there is a need to introduce a legal regulation that offers the opportunity to end the unbearable sufferings of children beyond human aid aged one to 12 years at least in exceptional severe cases.

In his letter of the 13th of October 2020[162], addressed to the Second Chamber of the States General the former Minister of Health, Welfare and Sport, Hugo de Jonge, member of the political party "Christian Democratic Appeal", stated that further reaching juridical safeguards for medical doctors are needed that offer them the opportunity to end the life of hopeless and unbearably suffering children in the age of 1–12 years.

The former Minister's intention was to prepare a respective legal regulation together with the Department of Public Prosecution and the regulatory bodies of the medical professions. It seems rather probable that a bill with the proposed content can also find enough support in the new parliament.[163]

Rise to the wish to develop the missing safeguards for medical doctors gave research, initiated in April 2016 by the former Minister of Health, Edith Schippers, who asked the Dutch Association for Paediatrics to investigate decision making and decisions around the end of life of children. The research was carried out at the University Medical Centres in Groningen, Rotterdam, and Amsterdam by Marije Brouwer and other researchers under the supervision of Eduard Verhagen, Professor of Paediatrics at Groningen University.[164] The focus of this research was directed to the group of children aged one to 12 years of age for whom active euthanasia still is generally prohibited. Subject of the research was the present practice of medical decisions about the end of life of these children. In the

---

161 M. Brouwer et al., Medische Beslissingen rond het Levenseinde bij Kinderen (1-12) 28-09-2019, 1 b.

162 Beleidsreactie Medische Beslissingen rond het levenseinde van kinderen 1-12 jaar, 13-10-2020.

163 A.-M. van der Kaaden, NRC/Handelsblad, 15-10-2020.

164 M. Brouwer et al., Medische Beslissingen rond het Levenseinde bij Kinderen (1-12), levenseindeonderzoekkind@umcg.nl

centre of the research stood the opinions of the parents and the paediatrics who treated children who suffered hopelessly and unbearably.

The main results of the research[165] were. that

- there exists a grey zone between palliative sedation and active euthanasia in the sense that it is not clear what the exact rules in this area are,
- in few cases the hopeless and unbearable sufferings cannot be suppressed by regular methods,
- several of the parents and most of the interviewed paediatrics (32 of the 38 of the interviewed paediatrics) declared that active euthanasia is needed as a last means for very severe cases,
- there was no signal found that children younger than 12 years were asking for euthanasia themselves and
- parents experienced a taboo, when talking about active euthanasia and often also about other means of ending life.

The research resulted in several recommendations, mainly the following:[166]

- Many paediatricians asked for a possibility to get palliative expertise in connection with respective decisions they must take. The recently founded support post of the Dutch Knowledge Centre Palliative Care for Children, might be the right instance to be a help as well for paediatricians as for parents confronted with palliative treatment.
- To clarify the differences between palliative sedation and active ending of life both concepts should be better defined. This can be realised in connection with the update of the guideline "Palliative Care for Children" of the Dutch Association for Paediatrics, that started in 2019.
- Many parents held the opinion that they were not sufficiently involved in the decision making concerning the end of life of their children. Many paediatricians were convinced that the parents often assess the situation of their children quite well, even what concerns the need of life lengthening means.
- There exist, communication -, organisation -, and decision-making problems, problems around the attention for family and child and concerning the problems about the pain relief. More knowledge is needed in all these areas. One of the recommendations therefore was to improve the education of all who

---

165 M. Brouwer et al., Medische Beslissingen rond het Levenseinde bij Kinderen (1-12), 4 a.
166 M. Brouwer et al., Medische Beslissingen rond het Levenseinde van Kinderen (1-12), 4 b.

participate in the palliative care for children. In 2018 the Knowledge Centre Palliative Care for Children was founded that according to the researchers should develop to the leading and directing organisation for palliative care for children and its improvement.

- There is according to the opinions of parents and paediatricians need to extend the possibilities of active euthanasia for the small group of children, who must suffer for a relatively long time but do not need life lengthening means and those whose process of dying will be long lasting and combined with very severe suffering. One estimates, that in the Netherlands it concerns about 5–10 children yearly.[167]

12. Summary of the recent developments in the Netherlands

Overviewing the years from 2017 to 2021 we can conclude that there was no total standstill, however, there was also no real progress in the search for a solution for the open questions in connection with euthanasia. The Supreme Court improved the situation by clarifying the premisses of euthanasia in cases of dementia, the Royal Dutch Medical Association by stressing the fact that medical doctors are not at all obliged to perform euthanasia, the "Perspective Research" by offering some new insights in the conditions of life, ideas, and feelings of people 55 years of age and older[168] who wish to end their lives. Furthermore, there was a slight opening into the direction of an acceptance of a right on suicide in the treatise of Den Hartogh[169] that, however, was almost immediately shut again in consequence of the supposed strength of the counterarguments, while a beginning was made with the development of a regulation to make euthanasia also accessible for hopeless and unbearable suffering children from one–12 years of age.

13. Excursus: The Corona Pandemic

2020 was the year dominated worldwide by the Corona Pandemic that is not yet defeated. At the end of 2020 about 100 million cases with more than 2 million deaths were registered in 190 countries. This pandemic is affecting all human rights, mainly, however the right to life. A pandemic as the Corona one even

---

167 A.-M. van der Kaaden, NRC/Handelsblad., 15-10-2020.
168 Els van den Wijngaarden et al. 2020.
169 Den Hartogh, NJB 2020, p. 2136.

forces us to accept a need of certain limitations of human rights. If we do that, we must answer the question, what human rights restrictions can be permitted to fight the risks of sickness and deaths respectively, what restrictions can be accepted as still proportional? It is difficult to find the right answers to that question as "human right to life is vitally important, but there is also a human right to live".[170] The general opinion of UN human rights experts is that there are no exceptions with Covid-19: Everybody has the right to life-saving interventions.[171] However, in practice, many states have difficulties to ensure that all their inhabitants live with security and dignity as Covid-19 continues to spread quickly and at the same time produces even more dangerous mutations. As far as circumstances are beyond our control as in the case of this pandemic, one cannot demand more than what is possible. Anyhow, the life-saving interventions, as far as they can be offered, must be inclusive of all groups of inhabitants and may not be discriminatory. In the Netherlands, this principle led to heavy discussions about the question to whom the last Intensive Care beds should be contributed if there were more patients needing them than beds available. This discussion circled mainly about the question whether selections may be based on the factor age when there are several patients with about the same chance to survive. The leading opinion so far is that in the first place, medical reasons should decide who is to be chosen. Next, those who need the Intensive Care treatment only for a short time and persons infected with the virus while working as medical doctors and nursing staff should be preferred. After these groups, a selection based on age can be made. The reasons given based on theoretical reflections so far are that choosing the youngest means that those were selected who so far had spent only relatively few years of life and that in this way, most years of life can be saved.[172]

In practice, however, things are handled differently, probably mainly because there is not enough time to find the answers to the questions that should be answered one for one precisely. It is a matter of fact that it is much more difficult and time-consuming to look after medical reasons than looking up the age.

Furthermore, there seems to exist a conspicuous difference between the recommendations the Royal Dutch Medical Association gives in her guidelines

---

170   Sarah Joseph, Griffith University, Australia, https: The conversation. com /COVID-19, risk and rights: the "wicked" balancing act for governments, 15-09-2020.
171   UN HRC, News and Press Release, 26-03-2020.
172   F. Weeda, Toch selectie op leeftijd voor een plek op de intensieve care, NRC/Handelsblad, 12-01-2021, In het Nieuws, p. 6.

about the necessity that doctors talk already early in advance and fully about the end of life with their patients and with the patient's families and what for so far seems to be in use in daily practice.[173] The increase of the Corona infections that cause relatively many deaths let the number and the importance of these conversations grow in number and at the same time also the number of possible mistakes. Not so long ago the following happened in a Dutch hospital: While visiting her husband, a wife wondered that her husband did not get anything to eat and to drink at lunchtime and she asked the nurse what the reason was. The nurse answered truthfully, saying: "The reason is that he is lying here just to die." This was an immense shock for the woman, who was still convinced that her husband would probably recover. Nobody had told her that a fatal end was not to prevent and so near by.

This example makes obvious how heteronomous determined the end of life still for people in hospital can be. Circumstantial evidence in this direction are also the suggestive formulations doctors often choose, when talking about these matters with the patient together with the family after they had spoken with their patients alone. Referring to the earlier conversation alone with the patient, a doctor, for example, asked the patient while the family was present: when talking about your treatment recently, didn't you say that it all makes no sense for you anymore? It is not only necessary that doctors talk with the patients and the family in time, they should talk with them also before they decide, what they must do. Hearing doctors talking with their patients, one sometimes has the impression, that they had already taken their decision before they addressed the patient, and now, talking with him or her, the conversation mainly has the task to get the agreement.

Only exceptionally, a patient will be able to change the doctor's mind. The situation is clear: here the ill and tired patient, lying in bed and there the sound self-confident physician, the expert, standing at the edge of the bed: The predominance is great. The Royal Dutch Medical Association (KNMG) asks its members regularly to speak in good time with the patients to prevent disappointments, incomprehension, and feelings to be too late to take important decisions.

At present, in hospital in the unit for Corona patients, there exist regularly only two options, the so-called "comfort version", an unpleasant word for what it describes, the ending of a human life as far as possible quickly and without

---

173 www.knmg.nl/advies-richtlijnen/dossiers/praten over het levenseinde, 11-06-2020; KNMG. Korte checklist voor artsen met bespreekpunten over levenseind (2017), KNMG, Praten over het levenseinde, Dossier, 11 juni 2020.

sufferings or the version with "life lengthening" treatments, which generally last longer, possibly include more pain, but can also possibly lengthen life and in few cases can even end in recovery. The doctor's descriptions of the two versions indicate clearly what the best is for the patient, generally the "comfort version". The wishes of the patient and of the family have not much influence on the choice finally made. Here again, the natural predominance of the physician, the expert, is influential, but also the question at what time the physician talks with the patient, is an important factor, on which mostly the physician decides alone.

If we think of the strength with which the life of those is protected who have the intense free will to end their life, but are not allowed to die in a humane way and we compare this situation with the relative easiness with which life of Corona patients at present is ended "with comfort", while they often want to stay alive and don't even always know that they were already given up, the discrepancy is surprising.

Probably, the Corona Pandemic is the main reason for the present situation, in which the right on life and human dignity are sometimes not only in danger, but probably already infringed.

In relation to the still strict protection of the life of those who have the free will to take their own lives, we find a growing extent of palliative sedation in the Netherlands that is about 10% higher than in other countries. According to the Dutch Monitor Palliative Care 2018[174], in 22,6 % of the cases of people who were dying during the last 7 years, the number of patients who got palliative care doubled. Information about the reason for this growing number seems to be not available. However, in the Monitor, the cost factor of treatment during the end-of-life phases and of palliative care plays an important role and of course, the length of the end-of-life phase has great influence on its costs. In the Monitor 2018, the opinions of the patients and their families did not belong to the subjects focussed on during the data collection. The next Monitor Palliative Care is planned for 2023.

An important question in connection with the Covid-19 patients is, whether they have a chance to survive and even to recover without an intensive care treatment in hospital, in a nursery home or even at home. Accordingly, the question rises whether and in how far instead of the "comfort version" in hospital a treatment in a nursery or at home with a nurse could be an alternative to save more lives. We found a certain general answer to this question in the registrations of

---

174 Stichting Farmaceutische Kerngetallen 2018, Pharmaceutisch Weekblad 2018, jaargang 153, no. 39.

the "Ysis", a system where a part of the Dutch nursery homes registrate Covid-19 patients. There were 629 patients registered as probably dying in consequence of a Corona infection, while 358 of the Corona patients recovered. These figures are not complete at all, but nevertheless circumstantial evidence of the fact that even in nursery homes about one third of the Corona patients, probably those with milder syndromes, survived.[175]

As everyone has the right to life-saving intervention, it is necessary to safeguard that Covid-19 patients are treated accordingly. Empirical research is necessary to get insight into the practice of diagnosing those, whom a "treatment with comfort" is recommended, but also concerning the quality of information they got and the time it took place. Patients have a right to know the state of their health, what the respective prognosis is, and to choose the treatment they prefer. Physicians generally need for every treatment, except in cases of emergency, the consent of the patient, and they must give all information the patients need to be able to decide, also about the treatment "with comfort". The word is misleading. It can include, as practice by now and then disclosed, intensive suffering and an end without the possibility to say farewell to the beloved.

If a patient and his or her family have doubts about what the doctors are planning, they should demand to stop the treatment. Sometimes, perhaps at present more often, this demand will come too late, as the process of dying was already started and cannot be redone without remaining serious consequences. Therefore, if the physicians give no or not enough information, the patient and his or her relatives should take as quickly as possible the initiative for an in-depth conversation.

Generally, for Covid-19 patients, euthanasia is not an option. At the beginning of the infection, they do not suffer unbearable and hopeless and in a later state, the time to get euthanasia arranged, principally some weeks, becomes too short.

---

175 M. van de Wier, Waarom euthanasie niet gaat bij het nieuwe coronavirus (en wat dan wel kan), Trouw (daily newspaper), 21-04-2020.

Part 3 Open questions and a view of the prospects of the future

1. Facts and figures, important to find right answers

1.1. Excursus: Suicide and euthanasia in history, the lasting roots

In the Netherlands, until now the development of euthanasia was mainly determined by the wish to help people who want to end their life because they are suffering unbearably from pain in hopeless situations. The decisive thought and driving force behind euthanasia was until now the strong wish to offer help as an obligation, perhaps under certain conditions even experienced as a constraint, to fulfil the duties of humanity. A free will of individuals to decide in the frame of the prevailing morals and the law not only about their personal life but also about its end was not accepted. A consequence of this thinking that has its roots in a long tradition is that the general acceptance of euthanasia in society is essentially restricted to the aspects of compassion and mercifulness. In the past of the West, suicide in ethics and culture always has been met with strong rejection.

Since old days there exists the precept "Thou shalt not kill"[176],[177] in our culture, which has its roots in the two words[178]"not" and "kill". Based on the context in which it is used - God is addressing his people - the word used for killing (razach) most probably might have had a meaning that is nearest to the English word "murder" and not referring to every kind of ending a life. It points on an action against a human being belonging to the people of Israel that causes his or her death. Already in Exodus 20,13 and in Deuteronomium, the last book of the Thora, 5,17 a word with the meaning of "murder" was used to translate "razach"[179]. In Greece, the words are translated with "ou fonefseis" that also refers to "murder". In the English King James Bible, however, that has most authority for Christians in the English-speaking countries, the translation is "kill". The new translation of the bible for protestants into Dutch chose "moord", meaning murder, while in the Dutch translation used by the Roman Catholic Church "razach" was translated by the word "kill".

---

176 King-James-Bible.
177 See: The Holy Bible, The Religious Tract Society, 2. Exodus 20.13 and 5. Deuteronomy 17.
178 "Io thirzach" in the original, in Hebrew "rezach".
179 There exist several versions of transcribing.

In the 16th century the German protestant reformer **Martin Luther** translated the respective text into German using the word equivalent to "kill": "Du sollst nicht töten". In the explanation of this text, Luther is speaking of the "next" – that can be principaly everybody -, as the person who may not be killed.

In the Bible, there is dealt with 10 cases of suicide, nine of them belong to the Old Testament. Nowhere in the Bible God forbids men to kill themselves, nowhere in the Bible suicide is condemned.[180] In the old text of the Bible as a whole, suicide is not clearly dealt with.[181] Accordingly it is not sure without any doubt whether "rezach" includes taking one's own life. As in the Old Testament death penalties are imposed for several crimes, for example for murder and kidnapping, the ban on killing of men was not absolute in this part of the Holy Bible. In the New Testament, killing is not allowed.[182]

In the opinion of Seneca, 62 after Christ, those who enjoyed life should live, and those who did not enjoy it could return to where they came from.[183]

For the Jews God as the creator of the world is the only one who can spend life and can take it away. Those who committed suicide had to be buried outside the churchyard as criminals without the usual mourning rituals. In Israel suicide was punishable until 1966.

In classical antiquity there existed different opinions about suicide. In addition to what was already pointed out in our Preface above we can add that the philosopher **Hegesias** of Cyrene taught that man is not at all able to achieve happiness and therefore should above all strive to prevent pain and sorrow. **Cicero** reported about him that he wrote a book on "Death by Starvation", a subject still of interest in modern times and quoted by Den Hartogh, too in his above cited article published in the Netherlands Law Journal in 2020. Hegesias got so much attention with his book that he was no longer allowed to teach in Alexandria.

In Roman times the protection of life by rejection of suicide was not strict. In the Roman Empire suicide was accepted as a natural right of free people.

The high society used the saying that "life is as a stage play that one can leave when it gets boring or unpleasant". **Seneca** hold the opinion that the freedom

---

180 Ferdinand von Schirach, Gott, Ein Theaterstück, Luchterhand, München 2020, p. 86-87.
181 K.-P. Jörns, in: Roman Herzog, Hermann Kunst et al., Evangelisches Staatslexikon 1987, I. Theologisch.
182 Ferdinand von Schirach, Gott, 2020, p. 89 etc.
183 Ferdinand von Schirach, Gott, 2020, p. 88.

of man to be able to decide on the own life and death had the highest significance,[184] while **Cicero** held the view that the need to protect human existence lies in nature.

In Christianity, **Augustine** (354–430) seems to have been the first who interpreted in his "De Civitate Dei", dating from 420 after Christ, the "Thy shalt not kill", referring to **Plato**, in the sense that this commandment also includes the protection of the own individual life.

Following the Jews, the Church later also introduced the rule that those who killed themselves could not be buried in consecrated earth. By now and then, however, exceptions were made as for example in the case of the famous professor Caspar van Baerle, better known as **Barlaeus**, who rather probably committed suicide, the exact circumstances were not thoroughly exercised, but nevertheless was buried in the famous New Church of Amsterdam.

An important argument against suicide for Catholics still is that life is a present of God that man may not refuse. Only since the Codex Iuris Canonici of 1983, suicide is no longer mentioned as a reason for exclusion from a church funeral.

For the protestant German reformer **Martin Luther** (1483–1546) suicide was the work of the devil.

During the Middle-Ages in many European countries suicide was punished as murder. The body was condemned to the gallows and to hang there for the raves or to be buried in a hole under a crossroads covered with chalk and pierced with a thick pin.

In the German Penal Code (Constitutio Criminalis Carolina) of 1532 suicide was not a punishable act, but this code was only in force subsidiarily to several penal law regulations in the different independent parts of the Holy Roman Empire of German Nation. In the Prussian Common Land Law [185] of 1794, we read that those who committed suicide should not be insulted or abused after their death. The Prussian Penal Code of 1851 does not mention suicide anymore.

For a long time, the confiscation of the fortune of those who committed suicide was common in Europe. An exception was made for mentally ill people.

Since the 18th century suicide was no longer punished in the Netherlands. This was about the same time that **Beccaria** categorized suicide as not being a secular crime, but a guilt that only God could punish after death. Beccaria also

---

184 Seneca, Epistulae morales ad Lucillum, https//de.wikipedia.org>Epistulae morales, Nr. 70.
185 Allgemeines Preussisches Landrecht.

argued against the confiscation of the fortune of those who had committed suicide reasoning that confiscation only punish the heirs, mostly the wife and the
children of the dead.

In the United Kingdom (UK) neither the argument that one is not allowed
to take one's own life because it was a present of God, nor the argument of the
existence of a responsibility versus community, was dominant as reason to make
suicide a criminal act, although these reasons might have been also influential.
In the UK, suicide was generally punishable and the reason for this fact was that
in cases of suicide **the Crown** loses one of its subjects, an argument that in times
of far-reaching overpopulation might no longer be of great importance. In the
UK suicide stayed punishable until 1961.[186]

As well in Catholicism as in Protestantism suicide, taking one's own by God
given life, was and still is a sin, which causes anathematization and excommu-
nication. As the core of religion is to believe it is not necessary to reason or
even prove it rationally. However, recently also in Protestantism the proposal
was made to make assisted suicide possible as a last means after all possibilities
of prevention had no success.[187] Until now, this is not at all the ruling opinion in
the German Protestant Church, but nevertheless, a small step in the direction of
more liberalisation was set.

Until present days, the influence of the main churches on the Dutch public
opinion concerning suicide is still present but losing its strength. The reason is
that many people are no longer attracted by the churches and in consequence the
Christian churches already lost about half of their members: **In 1975,** still 38% of
the Dutch population were Catholics and 33% Protestants while 26% had no religion. The respective figures for **2018** were: 22% Catholics, 15% Protestants, 53%
without religion, and 5% Muslims, who in 1975 still were a small minority. This
run away of members forced the churches to rethink many questions and to become more modest and careful concerning their demands versus their believers.

During the long period in which the Christian churches were powerful a culture developed that was strongly influenced by and mixed with their dominant
religious ideas. The ten words, sayings or in the words of the Geneva Bible the
ten commandments, were for centuries the fundamental principles related to
ethics, which were mainly taught and realized by the Church. Various rites and
festivities helped to integrate Biblical principles into daily life and older existing
traditions. Through the centuries a culture originated in which the population

---

186 Gerry Holt, When Suicide was Illegal, www.bbc.co.uk/news/magazine - 14374296.
187 www.evangelisch.de/personen/ulrich-lilie-0 /Diakonie Deutschland.

internalized Christian thought in a way that it became normal and principally beyond doubt. While, through centuries, churches lost by and by more influence on government and administration, at present they are losing their influence on the people. Therefore, at present old and new ethical principles are mainly regulated and enforced by law and jurisdiction that are accepted and internalized by the people independently from dogmas, but perhaps less strongly than under the influence of the church with their strict rules and controlling systems that brought much pressure on the believers.

The many centuries of antique philosophical thinking, humanism and religious faith all left their traces in present Western culture, not only in conscious thinking but probably more intensely in the unconscious existence. It belongs not only to the nature but also to the cultural heritage of mankind that there exists a strong aversion on suicide.

The fact that the religious political parties were so influential in connection with the establishment of the government programme for Rutten III was not their strength as big parties with many voters, but the special constellation of the high number of political parties that offered the Christian political parties not only the possibility to participate in government, but also to force the other members of this government to accept some of their conditions, mainly those related to euthanasia and suicide.

Since the period of the Enlightenment the freedom of responsible individuals to take their own decisions concerning their own life independently was growing. The protection of human life is no longer only theocratically regulated, but also by positive law. While step by step thought and knowledge of man steadily developed in many disciplines, also concerning the subject suicide, not at least in natural and medical sciences, but also in law, we notice the growing of rational views and correspondingly of the understanding of the problems combined with life and death. The possibilities, research can offer and the advantages of interdisciplinarity are not exhausted. With the further growing of our knowledge the rational basis of decision making might get stronger. It is possible that the views will become more liberal within the foreseeable future, but until now this question remains open.

1.2. Present knowledge about human life and death in natural science and psychology in a nutshell

Based on natural sciences, life, and death, both are defined assuming the fact that human life is characterized by consciousness. Particularly in human life individuals can experience their life, have the possibility to perceive the self and others and are able to act rationally and personally deliberately. According to ruling medical doctrine, if no brain functions are acting any more and the individual can no longer experience his own life, personality and life ended.[188] However, this opinion is not shared by all scientists.

There exist mainly three different aspects of consciousness: Consciousness as the ability to behave integrated in relation to others, consciousness in the sense of knowledge, respectively the possession of cognitive abilities concerning the outside world and in relation to the own mental situation, a special kind of immediate perception and consciousness as "phenomenal consciousness", subjective feelings as emotions, pain, recognizing colours, hearing sounds, feeling desires etc. In connection with these aspects of consciousness still the most difficult problem is the explanation of its origin.

Since many centuries, the relation between body, mind and soul was eagerly discussed and in theories already several answers were formulated. Nevertheless, the final answers seem not to be found yet. Until now, neuroscience cannot explain sufficiently the physiology of consciousness.[189]

In psychology where consciousness also is an important concept, one focusses primarily on the whole of psychological situations and activities man experiences and on a special kind of immediate perception concerning these experiences, the so-called inner experience. Important research subjects are for so far sequences of events as awareness, perception, considering, thought, philosophizing and decision making, but here, too, several questions are still open. Although natural sciences including medicine and psychology were able to extend knowledge steadily, many things stay unknown or not fully explained. Natural sciences still can not offer a safe rational basis to answer the questions that rise in connection with a better understanding and treatment of suicide. Several results found and accepted as ruling opinion stay contentious as they could not be fully proved. The results already found in natural sciences, however, were not yet all accepted by and integrated in other sciences and legal regulations.

The fact that in natural sciences many open questions still exist about facts related to the wish to end one's life makes it difficult, if not impossible, to develop definite adequate rational answers in law.

---

188 Steigleder, Wann ist der Mensch tot? p. 103,
189 Wikipedia, Bewusstsein (18-08-2020).

1.3. Causes of suicide and euthanasia

In nature the basic principle is that all that lives strives to stay alife. Suicide is a negation of and an exception to this principle and readily calls the suspicion that there is something out of order in the life of the person who denies this principle.

Modern clinical psychology and psychiatry made obvious that suicide often is a result of psychological disorders, that principally could be prevented or cured at least partly.

In the Netherlands, so far, a bill was already prepared to amend the Law on Public Health for the purpose to support and anchor integral suicide prevention (Law on Integral Suicide Prevention).[190]

However, in many countries, those prevention means are still (2020) only exceptionally or even not at all available. Suicide has many reasons, it can be based on environmental, social, personal and/or interpersonal factors. Until now, the number of research results is still low and as suicide is affected by socio-cultural factors it is not easy to make use of research results found in other countries.

Quite interesting is a recently published longitudinal research project focussing on the question whether national suicide prevention programmes are effective.[191] The answer was positive: A decline was found in suicide rates in the verum countries (Norway, Sweden, Finland and Australia) in males with strongest effect of those between 25-44 and 45-64 years.

One of the positive results of the fact that the knowledge about the causes of suicide and the possibilities to treat them at least partly became better known through the years is, that the public became more understanding versus suicide. Furthermore, the better knowledge made that family and acquaintances who in the past often were blamed for the fact that they did not prevent the death of their relative or friend are no longer accused so much anymore. According to the World Health Organisation,[192] however, suicide still is stigmatising and a taboo, something that might be the heritage of the long history of constant rejection and condemnation.

When we think of the above cited Dutch empirical research initiated on basis of the coalition agreement 2017-2020 conducted by Els van den Wijngaarden et al. among people aged 55 years and older and the importance of psychological

---

190 Parliamentary Documents II 2020/21, 35 754, no .4.
191 U. Lewitzka, C. Sauer, M. Bauer, W. Felber, Are national suicide prevention programs effective? A comparison of 4 verum and 4 control countries over 30 years, BMC Psychiatry, 2019. https://doi.org/10.1186/s12888-019-2147-y
192 Who.int/newa-room, factsheets/detail/suicide, 2018.

and/or psychiatric disorders in cases of suicide, it is surprising that in this research the quantitative part (21,294 interviews) outnumbers the qualitative research (34, respectively 37 in-depth interviews) by so far.

About 50% of the cases of suicide are caused by depression. Other important
reasons are bipolar disorders, eating disorders, borderline personality disorders,
and schizophrenia. Further traumatic stress and post-traumatic stress disorder
can be of much influence. Use of drugs and alcoholics, loss, or fear to lose one's
wealth and social status, total hopelessness can intensify the risk. Chronical pain,
terminal illness, the fear of a long and painful illness and, also important, the
fear of loosing one's dignity are other important factors. Furthermore, the belief to be a burden for others and social isolation can contribute strongly to the
wish to commit suicide, as was also found in the Dutch research by Els Van den
Wijngaarden et al.[193]

Suicide can also be a cry for help, initiated only to arouse attention as, for
example, in the case of a well-known pianist who needed new engagements and
hoped for publicity in the media, but unfortunately the in advance organized
helper came not in time and he was found too late.

And then there are the many cases in which people end their life in consequence of their failures in social life, when, for example, the debts grow so high
that they never can be paid back and/or the heavy moral mistakes cannot be put
right again.

However, all possible causes for suicide do not necessarily lead to this deed.
For so far, those who commit suicide are not only victims of environmental factors, the society that does not allow them to find a humane end, but also of their
own physiology. Are they conditioned to fight for life or to flee from it?

As a high percentage of suicide is caused by disorders and misfortune, there
is hope, that with the use of more and better prevention means already now several suicide deaths can be anticipated and that in future the situation will further
improve after new means to cure the relevant illnesses and disorders are added
to the existing ones. However, the probability that there are remedies found for
all illnesses and disorders is not great as new illnesses will develop. Taking one's
own life is of all times and therefore the fact must be taken into consideration as
a decisive criterion of assessment that there are always people living in extreme
emergency situations in society who lost all hope and decide to end their life because they are missing the conditions needed to survive. If they are not able to
get the help and/or the respective lethal means freely, many of them will try to

---

193 Nancy Schimelpfening, Carly Snyder, www.verywellmind.com of 20-03-2020.

get them illegally, in their total despair search for help at dubious organizations and clubs[194] or meet a violent death with all its dreadful consequences for themselves, their family, third persons and society.

Many cases of suicide are not planned but committed impulsively and therefore difficult to prevent. In international research one also found certain indications, that suicide is related to phases of economic recession in society.

1.4. Suicide, euthanasia, and age

During the last 50 years the suicide rate increased world-wide to about one million a year with an average of 16 per 100,000 people.

During the last decennia research and studies on suicide as well as proposals and amendments of bills on this subject were mainly focusing on people of 55 years of age and older in The Netherlands. Suicide, however, can happen at quasi every age, but there are differences in quantity of cases. In 2019 there were altogether 1,811 cases of suicide registered in the Netherlands, 104 per one million inhabitants, the lowest number since 2012.[195] Most suicides were committed by people aged in their 50 s,[196] the group that was only partly included in the research of Els van den Wijngaarden et al. that was focussing on people aged 55 years and more.

The numbers of the groups of teeners and of people aged 60 years and older increased in 2019 by 16, respectively 614 persons in relation to the year before.[197]

In recent research on suicide among youths under 20 years of age in the Netherlands[198] related to the general population of youth, relatively higher suicide rates were found among male and older youths, youths living alone, and those being Dutch by descent.

---

194 M. Effting, H. Kraak, Ooggetuigen over een zelfgekozen dood met Middel X, de Volkskrant, 05-12-2021, Zaterdag, p. 6-10.

195 www.hartvannederland/nieuws 2020/aantal-zelfmoorden.

196 Suicide deaths per 100.000 population in the Netherlands in 2018 per age groups in %: Younger than 20 years 1.3 %, 20-30 years 10.1 %, 30-40 years 11.6 %, 40-50 13.0 %, 50-60 years 17.3 %, 60-70 years 14.3 %, 70-80 11.8 % and more than 80 years 13.8 %.

197 1811 zelfdodingen in 2019. www.cbs.nl (29-09- 2020).

198 G. Berkelmans, R. v. d. Mei, S. Bhulai and S. Merelle, Demographic Risk Factors for Suicide among Youths in the Netherlands, International Journal of Environmental Research and Public Health 2020, 17, 1182.

1.5. Dutch numbers of suicide in relation to some other countries

The numbers of suicide in the Netherlands are in relation to other countries moderate. That is an important fact of interest for the public discussion about this subject.

The suicide mortality rate, the number of suicide deaths in a year per 100,000 population from 2000 to 2020 (Macro Trends),[199] for example, were highest on the list in Belgium 20.70 and lowest in Antigua and Barbuda with 0.50. Here follow some more examples from high to low: Hungary 19.10, Japan 18.50, France 17.70, Austria 15.60, United States 15.30, Sweden 14.80, Portugal 14.00, Germany 13.60, the Netherlands 12.60, United Kingdom 8.90, Spain 8.70, Italy 8.20, Israel 5.40, Greece 5.00, and Saudi Arabia 3.20. What concerns the last three cited countries, is surely religion rather influential.

Based on the above Macro Trends, in the Netherlands yearly about 2,000 people commit suicide.

1.6. Suicide by gender

In the Netherlands there are about twice as many men as women succeeding in committing suicide. In 2019 of the totally 1,811 suicide deaths, there were 1,232 men and 579 women. What concerns thinking about suicide and making respective plans, however, there are no significant differences in numbers, but the attempts of women are less successful than those of men. Their attempts relatively more often end in hospital or at a First Aid Post.

1.7. Methods of taking one's own life

There are many methods to commit suicide. The predominant methods are hanging, poisoning by pesticide, and shooting with firearms. Also frequently used are jumping from high, using a drug overdose and drowning. The methods differ between men and women, the latter preferring the "softer", not so bloody means, but there are also differences between countries and cultures.

In the Netherlands about 10% of the suicides are railway related. In Germany, this percentage is 7%, about three railway related suicides per day. The real victims of this kind of suicide are the traumatized train drivers. The Deutsche Bahn (German Railways) organizes special treatments for these train drivers who

---

199 https://www.macrotrends.net,

suffer from post traumatic stress disorders in a specialized hospital in Malente, a city in Northern Germany. The death rate of railway related suicide is one in two attempts! The damages of health of those who survive are often terrible. In the Netherlands, in Germany and other countries there are various prevention means used, such as signs by light or sound and special constructions to act against railway -, subway - and other traffic-related suicide attempts, causing various dangers, high costs, and victims who for the rest of their life are handicapped and in need of help.

Before making comments about suicide and euthanasia and even more before passing a judgement about these subjects one should know as much as possible about the relevant facts. Aspects that seem to be not sufficient enough taken into consideration are the enormous predicaments in connection with which suicide is performed, situations that are relatively often long-lasting and causing extreme sufferings for the people who commit suicide under horrible circumstances because they are not allowed to end their life in a humane way, but also for their families and friends, for all those who become involved in these acts just by chance or in connection with their occupational tasks. It is the corpse that tells us in every single case how terribly they suffered and their fate blames society for its harshness, lack of understanding, humanity, and compassion.

However, not many people in society are able to recognize the connections of occurrences that led to the death of those people. If more people would be better informed, the public opinion would probably be different. It was already in the second year of my study at Hamburg University that I attended the course Forensic Medicine for Law Students during which we also had to attend forensic post-mortem examinations during which questions of importance for law cases were presented, for example, questions whether the death of a person was natural, a suicide or the result of a crime. Many cases were for various reasons deeply distressing. One of them was especially impressing by the persistence with which it took place. A man in the forties committed again and again several attempts before he finally succeeded by jumping from a mooring post. Every time, before he jumped into the river Elbe, he put a thick rope around his neck, fastened it on the post, and bound heavy stones on his feet to keep him long enough under water. From the many scars and wounds on his body the forensic physicians could precisely reconstruct what happened before he died, the number of attempts, he made, the approximate time between these attempts, that were weeks and months, the extreme sufferings he had to undergo before he finally was dead. Those who decided to end their life and tried it without success, mostly do not stop before they reach their aim. Has society the right to let these dreadful kinds of acts of despair consciously happen in the name of the prevention of potential dangers for elderly people who might be initiated to flee life being convinced to be a burden for others? Are there not various other possibilities to prevent this potential danger?

The fact that suicide still is a taboo theme and euthanasia is only in exceptional cases accepted, results also in the consequence that many people who commit suicide are not sufficiently informed about the most effective means for a calm end and how they work, is another reason for dramatic shocking events.

Empirical research so far confirms that free access to lethal means causes the risk that the number of cases of suicide increases.

2. Suicide, and euthanasia, right, and law

2.1. The Dutch Constitution

The present Constitution for the Kingdom of the Netherlands directly derives from the Constitution of 1815. In 1948 a revision introduced parliamentary democracy and in 1983 an even more comprehensive revision took place. Nevertheless, the Dutch Constitutions is regarded as one of the oldest still in use. The Dutch Constitutional tradition is rather sober. There is a reference to "Human Dignity" missing.

In the Netherlands until now, not sufficiently broad, and open discussion about the question took place, whether, respectively to what extent, there exists for all sound of mind responsible people of age a right to decide about the end of their own life. So far, the Dutch Supreme Court did not deal with this question although there were opportunities to go into the problem concerning the autonomy of men.[200] The prevailing opinion seems to be that the right of self-determination is not the main carrying principle of the "Termination of Life Review Act". This law rests, as the Dutch Supreme Court stated recently in its judgement of the **17th of December 2019**[201], at the same time on "the protection status of life, the right of self-determination of men, the compassion with those who suffer and the protection of human dignity". In connection with this statement the Dutch Supreme Court refers to the following legal regulations: The Right to Life (Art. 2 European Convention on Human Rights, ECHR), the Right to Freedom from Torture and Inhuman or Degrading Treatment (Art. 3 ECHR) and the Right of Respect for Private and Family Law (Art. 8 ECHR). In the same

---

200 S. Bolte-Knol, Geen terughoudende rol van het strafrecht bij de beoordeling van euthanasiezaken, NJB 2020, p. 1456 etc., p. 1458/9.
201 Nr. 19/04910, ECLI:NL:2020:712.

judgement the Dutch Supreme Court stressed the fact that the jurisdiction of the European Court of Human Rights offers the member states a relative wide discretional competence concerning the decision how they want to protect the life of patients in hopeless situations.

In the first place it might be surprising that the Dutch Supreme Court, the highest National Court of the Netherlands, did not choose a national legislation, primarily the Dutch Constitution, but internationally accepted legal principles and the European Convention on Human Rights to summarize what the fundamental principles of Dutch Law on Euthanasia are. Why did the Supreme Court make this choice? Reading the first part of the Dutch Constitution, in which the "Fundamental Rights" are summarized in 23 articles, one realizes that the norms and values highlighted by the Supreme Court as the basis of the Termination of Life Review Act, the protection status of life, the right to self-determination, the protection of human dignity, and compassion with those who suffer, are not all fully regulated in extension in the catalogue of Fundamental Rights of the Dutch Constitution. So important subjects as human dignity and self-determination are not literary named. Accordingly, the Fundamental Rights in the First Part of the Netherlands Constitution alone do not answer the presently so important questions about the extend and significance of Human Rights for individuals to decide on their own life and death.

In art. 11 the Dutch Constitution explicitly protects "The Inviolability of the (Human) Body" and in Article 10 "Privacy". Human Life as such and its end are not defined.

Most articles belonging to the Fundamental Rights of the Dutch Constitution concern the rights, individuals have as members of society and the rights existing between people. Although the European Convention on Human Rights regulates certain aspects of Human Rights more detailed than the Dutch Constitution, it too, does not answer the question whether and in how far man may decide on his own life's end.

In the Dutch Constitution we find no answer to the question whether dying the natural way belongs to the protection of life by Article 11 Dutch Constitution titled "Inviolability of the (Human) Body". Furthermore, there is no answer to the question whether individuals have a right to end their life in a humane way on basis of their own free will. Can the absence of this answer be understood in another way than as a negation? A result of this ban is that in the Netherlands yearly about 2,000 people decide to end their life in an inhumane, often cruel way.

During the last centuries one tried to improve the situation of those who had lost their courage to go on living mainly by developing various prevention means and by helping them at least as a last resort to some extent to end their live in a more humane way, introducing new legal regulations, primarily the Termination of Life Review Act.

It is a matter of fact, that at present, a growing number of people in the Netherlands attach much value on the right of self-determination. They want to decide themselves and do not want to be dependent of the opinion or judgement of others. The same is true for what concerns the end of life. The great majority of people nowadays want to decide themselves and do not want to follow up the decision taken by others. In **2019**, according to research of the Dutch Central Bureau for Statistics[202], 55% of the Dutch population declared that euthanasia should be possible for those who are weary of life, while 32% of the population did not share this opinion.[203]

Therefore, the question rises, whether meanwhile the time has not come to work out more detailed contents of so important rights as "Human Dignity" and "Self-determination" with their significance for human life and death. This legislative work should be done in an interdisciplinary frame based on the opinion of the majority in the Netherlands and on Dutch law thinking, striving to develop clear concepts for the First Part of the Dutch Constitution. Reading the European Convention on Human Rights makes obvious that a national legal regulation can not only fit better with the national legal system but can also offer the possibility for a more detailed specific regulation than a legislation that must be accepted by many countries with varying legal cultures that consequently can be only a compromise solution generating the lowest common denominator as the result.

At present, public interest in the Constitution with its Fundamental Rights is strong and growing. The fundamental rights are cited increasingly in public discussion to prove the right of certain ideas and opinions. In these discussions, however, the contents of fundamental law concepts are not always cited and interpreted correctly, sometimes they are even misused. This fact makes obvious, how important it is to develop clear concepts with exact definitions for the fundamental rights in general, and especially as basis for a broad and open discussion that is needed to shape the public opinion of the majority concerning the question to what extent individuals have the right to decide about their own life and death.

---

202 Centraal Bureau voor de Statistiek (CBS).
203 R. Oosterom, M. v. d. Wier, Trouw (Newspaper), 31-01-2020.

2.2. Human diversity, human dignity, and the need of self-determination

In law objective facts and abstract concepts are of fundamental importance. Equity of people, for example, is an essential principle for a democratic state. However, in nature there exist many differences everywhere and men differ in many regards and in various extents. Individuals are very variable in many ways and that must be taken into consideration not at least for reasons of humanity. What and how an individual thinks, can be at least roughly understood by other individuals so far as it was clearly expressed by speaking or writing of people who belong to the same or a similar culture. But what other people perceive, feel, detect, notice, discern, believe, other individuals generally can recognize only partly, depending on the concrete social intercourse, but hardly ever totally, respectively. Everybody has his or her individual emotions and understanding of his or her dignity, depending on the individual personality, every individual has his or her own physiological and psychological structures that cause emotions, thoughts, and behaviour which are not easy to empathize, share, comprehend and reconstruct by others. Every human being is unique. How much, for example, do we really know about, and in how far are we able to understand and to feel with a partner we live together since years? Can we empathize his or her pain, the sufferings caused by his or her losses and the distress that is not ours? If the feelings of individuals differ in kind and intensity so much, can mutual understanding then be other than only by approximation? Can a physician, who generally meets his patients only by now and then for a relatively short time really "diagnose" exactly the sufferings they undergo? If not, makes it sense to let the findings of the medical doctor in so far prevail the perceptions and the will of the person who suffers?

The existence of a great diversity of people who all should have equal rights is a fact that makes it necessary to create and guarantee the freedom for everybody to live in accordance with his or her individual needs, as far as this does not restrict others in their rights. Accordingly, there should be space for various models of life, for every ego the one to preserve his or her uniqueness, and dignity, based on the respective own individual rational understanding and emotional perception.

Excursus: Musing about the reality of the existence of such **a great diversity of people** with a discrepancy between self-perception and the perception of others, one can add that there is everywhere on earth in nature an immense splendid diversity. If there exists a divine creation, must this variety then not be a part of this divine creation, which is inhabited by individuals who are endowed with intellect, talents, inspiration, the strive for self-determination and self-realisation, as one can observe and experience continuously while participating?

2.3. The German Constitution, human dignity, and an unwritten right on self-determination

2.3.1. The German Constitution

After the end of the Second World War with all its many atrocities[204], a new Constitution for Germany[205] was worked out on the instruction of the three Western Occupying Powers by the German Parliamentary Council.[206] In this way the Parliamentary Council got the opportunity to correct the weak points in the Constitution, in force during the Weimar Republic, and to add modern Human Rights regulations that are based on the idea of Human Dignity. This German Constitution, the Basic Law, came into force in May 1949. The Universal Declaration of Human Rights[207] (UDHR) was proclaimed by the United Nations General Assembly in Paris only some months before.[208] The first article of the UDHR reads:" All human beings are born free and equal in dignity and rights. They are endowed with reason and conscience and should act towards one another in a spirit of brotherhood." The first article of the German Basic Law[209] states: "Human dignity shall be inviolable. To respect and protect it shall be the duty of all state authority."[210] In this way human dignity was placed at the top of the German Basic Law and at the same time at the top of the whole German legal system, directly followed by the Human Rights. Although human dignity was placed in the German Basic Law before the part on Human Rights, according to the opinion of the German Federal Constitutional Court and most German legal experts, Human Dignity also is the most important Human Right.

The emphasis of human dignity in the German Basic Law has no model in other constitutions and there are several constitutions, so as for example, the Dutch Constitution, that do not mention dignity at all. The main reason that especially human dignity is stressed so strongly in the present German Basic Law

---

204 With worldwide about some 75 million deaths, https://en.wikipedia.org>wiki>World War II.
205 Constitution of 23 May 1949, Federal Law Gazette (Bundesgesetzblatt) 1949, Nr. 1, p. 1.
206 Parlamentarischer Rat.
207 UDHR, https://www.un.org/sites/un2.org/files/udhr.pdf
208 On 10-12-1948.
209 Grundgesetz (GG).
210 Art. 1, sub 1

is that human dignity and human rights were so extremely ignored and violated during the Third Reich. The importance of human dignity for the German legal system is also stressed by the fact that Art. 1 Basic Law is subject to Art. 79 sub 3 Basic Law, the so-called eternity clause, that regulates for certain articles of the Basic Law that constitutional amendments are not permitted.

For the first time human dignity was mentioned in a German constitution in the Weimar Constitution of 1919 in connection with the regulation of economy where the phrase "conditions in conformity with human dignity for all human beings"[211] was used.

Human dignity is neither defined in the Universal Declaration of Human Rights, nor in the EU Convention for the Protection of Human Rights and Fundamental Freedoms, and in the German Constitution.

A detailed definition would be difficult to develop for so many and diverse ideas, and an open concept has several advantages in view of the extent of the concept and the many changes it is regularly influenced by. When the German Basic Law was introduced shortly after the end of the Second World War the maxim "Die Würde des Menschen ist unantastbar"[212] surely affected the people more and in a different way than at present. Since the German Basic Law came into force, there changed a lot in the consciousness and the ideas of the general-public, and in the linguistic usage, too. Perhaps, meanwhile the word "dignity" for modern young people got even a somewhat pathetic note.

Roots of dignity are found in religion. According to Christianity, Islam and Judaism, God created man in his own image[213] and therefore all people hold a certain value that just belongs to their being human. This value, dignity, is tied inseparable to the existence of man and it is this natural human dignity that justifies the existence of human rights.

For a view on human dignity as it was understood in the period the German Basic Law was introduced, the explanation given by Günter Dürig[214] is of special interest. Still at present it can serve as a basis to summarize the content of dignity in connection with law.

As generally in modern times, also Dürig based human existence on the virtue of man's spirit, that enables him to become aware of himself, to determine

---

211 Ein menschenwürdiges Dasein.
212 Human dignity shall be inviolable.
213 Genesis 1, 27.
214 Theodor Maunz/Günter Dürig, Commentary on the Basic (Constitutional) Law of Germany, Art. 1 Abs, 1 Rn.17/Erstb. Beck, München, 1958 etc.

himself, and to shape himself and his environment. These abilities and based on them, self-confidence, autonomy, lack of heteronomy, self-responsibility, self-design, and self-organisation offer man freedom and equality.

In present German law and legal practice, there exists an interaction between human dignity and the human right to live one's own life.[215] Based on the two first articles of the Basic Law, Art. 1 sub 1 (Human Dignity) and Art. 2 sub 1 (Right to Live one's own Life) a General Right of Personality was developed by jurisdiction, the right of self-determination that is not explicitly regulated in German written law (legislation), but generally recognized in legal practice.[216]

When the German Basic Law was introduced so shortly after the end of the Second World War with worldwide about 70 million deaths, the protection of human life and human dignity was by far the outstanding object that must be protected. In those days, a broad public discussion about a right to end life self-determined, still was far away.

At present, the first two articles of the German Constitution together with the general Right of Self-determination are the legal basis for the courts to decide, among other things, cases concerning the right to live one's own life until its end. At present, for Dutch judges a comparable basis does not exist.

2.3.2. The judgment of the German Federal Constitutional Court on § 217 German Criminal Law

An important example for recent German jurisdiction on the complex of themes of the present study, based on the Basic Law and the unwritten right of self-determination is the judgement of the Second Senate of the German Federal Constitutional Court in which the Senate had to decide about the constitutionality of the by then new § 217 German Criminal Code in which the business-like support of help in connection with suicide was made punishable. In this judgment of the **26th of February 2020** concerning the right to live one's own life at

---

215 Das Allgemeine Persönlichkeitsrecht, Art. 2, 1 and 2 Basic Law:
 (1) Every person shall have the right to free development of his personality insofar as he does not violate the rights of others or offend against the constitutional order or the moral law.
 (2) Every person shall have the right to life and physical integrity. Freedom of the person shall be inviolable. These rights may be interfered with only pursuant to a law.

216 "Gewohnheitsrechtlich anerkannt".

the end of life,[217] the judges. among other things, stated clearly in the guiding principles of this judgment,

- that the General Right of Personality includes, stressing the personal autonomy, the Right to die self-determined (sub 1 a),
- that the General Right of Personality includes the freedom to take one's own life (sub 1 b) and
- that the freedom to take one's own life includes the freedom to make use of the help of third persons as far as this help is offered (sub 1 c).

The Second Senate of the German Federal Constitutional Court finally concluded that § 217 German Criminal Code was not in conformity with the Basic Law and accordingly invalid.[218]

With this judgment that fully corresponds with the spirit of the German Basic Law, characterized by its "Human dignity shall be inviolable", the German Federal Constitutional Court stated clearly, that, based on the General Right of Personality, there exists also at the end of life, a Right of Self-determination, that includes a right on a self-determined death.

However, this judgment does not answer all important questions that exist about a self-determined end of life. For example, the Federal Constitutional Court did not answer the regularly discussed[219] question, whether free access to lethal means should be allowed. And indeed, it is not the task of jurisdiction, but of the legislator to develop the law that gives the respective detailed answers in regulations that offer the people the certainty of law in the relatively narrow frame the Federal Constitutional Court offered for legislation in its judgment.

2.3.3. Two German draft-bills on suicide and suicide assistance

Until now, the German legislator did not fulfil this task, but recently mainly the following two bills concerning a Law on Suicide Assistance were introduced, one by members of three German political parties, the Socialists, the Liberals, and the Lefts[220]: "The Bill to Maintain and Enforce the Right of Self-determination

---

217 Bundesverfassungsgericht, Decision of the Federal Constitutional Court of 26-02-2020 – 2BvR 2347/15 -, Rn. 264.
218 In German law assisting a criminal act is principally only punishable so far as the criminal act itself is punishable. As suicide is not punishable, assisting suicide is principally not punishable, too.
219 See Part 2, 9.
220 https://dserver.bundestag.de/btd/19/286/1928691.pdf

at the End of Life", and one by "The Greens". Both are based on the above sum-marized judgement of the German Federal Constitutional Court of the 26th of February 2020 with which the Federal Constitutional Court offered the legislator the opportunity to regulate the proceedings of medical doctor assisted suicide. The bills will be discussed in parliament soon.

In the case of assisted suicide, one lets the person who wants to die have the lethal means, but they are not administered. This makes it for many suicides extremely difficult to realize the planned act because many of them need the help of somebody else, as we know from empirical research.[221]

In the draft bill on assisted suicide of the three political parties, mainly the following subjects are regulated:

1. The right to die self-determined
2. An obliged detailed consultation at an independent state-approved instance
3. The prescription of lethal means by physicians for use in connection with assisted suicide

Ad 1. Everybody who, based on an autonomously formed free will, wants to end life has the right to take advantage of the help of others (§ 1).

Everybody may help those who decided, based on an autonomously formed free will, to end their life.

Nobody can be obliged to help to commit suicide.

Nobody may be prohibited to help or to refuse help (§ 2).

An autonomously formed free will requires the ability to form this will freely and uninfluenced by an acute mental disturbance and to act in accordance with the respective insight. In general, according to the bill, these conditions do not exist before a person reaches the age of 18 years. Persons who want to end their life must be able to weight the pros and cons. Therefore, it is necessary that those who plan to end their life, are fully informed about all alternatives that are to their proposal.

A free will exists only so far as the decision to end life was taken without any attempt of influence or pressure by third persons. An autonomously formed free will can be only assumed if the wish to end life lasts for a certain period, and if it has a certain firmness. (§ 3).

Ad 2) Important precondition for the possibility to take one's own life is that a detailed consultation took place in advance. Everybody who permanently lives in Germany has the right to get advice and everybody who wants to commit

---

221 See above.

suicide must get an open, not trying to impose a will consultation immediately by an independent state-approved advice-centre. The consultation is free of costs. After the consultation, the advice-centre hands the person in question a written confirmation about the consultation. If the person who gave the advice has doubts about the voluntariness of the planned suicide, these doubts must be notified in the written confirmation (§ 4).

Paragraph 5 regulates the Advice Centres in detail.

Ad 3) Of special importance is paragraph 6 of the bill that allows medical doctors to prescribe lethal medications for suicides if the precondition of paragraph 3 of the bill, the autonomously formed free will to take one's life, exists. The bill intends to amend the Narcotics Act in a way that the prescription of Natrium-Pentobarbital becomes possible for use in connection with assisted suicide.

The medical doctor is obliged to inform the person in question about all the important medical circumstances for suicide, including the possibilities to cure a diagnosed disease and the possibilities of palliative medicine.

The physician must ask the customer for the written confirmation of the consultation that may not be older than eight weeks and must have taken place at least ten days ago to prove the firmness of the wish to die.

The bill on medical doctors assisted suicide of the members of "The Greens" was prepared by Renate Künast and Katja Keul. An important difference in relation to the above summarized bill is that it provides for a differentiation between people who are seriously ill and those who have other reasons to end their life. For the second group, the demands of seriousness and firmness are higher.[222]

The future of the two bills is uncertain. Probably a compromise will be found. After all, the Federal Constitutional Court did already accept the existence of a right to die self-determined and both bills did not include the difficult and very controversial discussed question how to decide in cases of persons suffering from dementia who wrote a patient decree in advance, when they still were not suffering from this disease. Therefore, the chance of acceptance of the proposed regulations by parliament might be relatively high. Nevertheless, the discussion will be intense as several details might be controversial:

Is the age of 18 years, when majority begins in Germany, the right choice? Is there not a more detailed regulation needed to consider special stages of age, for example, adolescence? And what about the period of 10 days to eight weeks after the obliged consultation? Is it always adequate? Should every physician be

---

222 taz.de, Gesetz zu Suizidassistenz, 30-01-2021.

allowed to hand out lethal means? Are physicians at all, whose profession is to save life and to cure people, the right persons to hand out the lethal means? Should there not be specially trained physicians for this task who develop a specialist opinion that could help to improve the range of alike treatment? At present, there seems to exist differences in treatment in practice, depending on the opinions of the respective physicians.

Both, the fact that there exist already organisations in Germany - and elsewhere in Europe - that offer medical doctors' assisted suicide generally for about € 10,000[223] and since many years well-known one-way journeys to Switzerland of people who hope to find a humane end of their life there, far away from home, surely will influence the law-making process.

2.4. Summing-up

In the Netherlands, meanwhile already for 20 years, the "Termination of Life on Request and Assisted Suicide Act 2001"[224] is in use and since July 2020 a bill on "Completed Life" is ready, waiting to be dealt with in parliament. Until now, neither in the Dutch Constitution nor in the Law on Euthanasia nor in the Completed Life Bill the general fundamental principles for legal regulations on the end of life were regulated in clear terms. In its judgement dating of the 17th of December 2019, the Dutch Supreme Court summarized as the respective main principles the protection of life, the right of self-determination of man, the compassion with those who suffer and the protection of human dignity. These principals are all of influence on legal practice, but they are only partly legally regulated, they have different standards and their relation to each other is not fixed. Therefore, the conclusion must be that regulations for practice for so far are missing.

In Germany, Human dignity and the right of personality are regulated in the Basic Law, while the right of self-determination only has the status of a principal that is generally recognized in legal practice. Accordingly, there rest several questions such as, what is the relation between human dignity, the right of personality and the right of self-determination (1) in connection with life and (2) in connection with the end of life? How should the term "end of life" be defined? Is the right of self-determination not a part of the right of personality? If it would belong to the right of personality, it would already possess a legal status. What

---

223 taz. (daily German newspaper, https://en.wikipedia.org), 30-01-2021, Sterbehilfe nur nach Beratung.

224 Above, Part 1. 3.

are the reasons that a respective regulation is not in force? Are the Human Basic Rights, as regulated in Art. 2 and the following articles of the Basic Law, not just explanations of the contents of "Dignity" to make them better applicable?

3. Taking one's own Life, Dementia, and Human Dignity

The subject taking one's own life and Dementia was already our topic above in connection with several aspects published in connection with research, jurisdiction, and law. What still is missing in this context is the significance of human dignity. There was already stated above, that the free will of man is the reason and the basis for self-determination and that human dignity is tied with man solely by the existence of men as human beings. Thus, nobody can take dignity away. Principally only persons sound of mind who possess a free will, are of age and responsible for their actions have the possibility to decide on taking their own life. In cases of advanced Dementia, these preconditions are not present. Then, however, the question rises, whether and in how far one can declare one's own will in advance, still possessing a sound mind, for the time one might be mentally retarded. There were different answers given to this question.

Fact is that mentally sound people relatively often change their mind. That is a consequence of the natural functioning of our brain that is continuously altered in consequence of all the new impressions and experiences men have. New connections are formed in brain, whereas old ones are strengthened or no longer used as our memory is not just the collection of the many experiences we had, but primarily the result of the transformation process in which the collected material is regularly revised and updated to make it better suitable for use in future.[225] Therefore, everything collected and summarized in our memory is not necessarily the same as it was when it was stored. Thus, the construction of our brain and the concept of its functioning are not predisposed to develop consistency. A consequence of the fact that human brain alters itself regularly in connection with inner and external developments is that man often changes his mind. That is also true for his will to live respectively to die. These wishes, too, are not consistent.

Also mentally retarded people are regularly influenced by their surrounding and their emotions and, as far as we know, they change their preferences, too, but often they are no longer able to understand what is going on and how to

---

225 J. Shaw, Das trügerische Gedächtnis, Wie unser Gehirn Erinnerungen fälscht, Carl Hanser Verlag, München, 2016.

declare their will sufficiently. Nevertheless, they principally are human beings with dignity.

Does human dignity permit us to end the life of a demented person, who at present is no longer able to declare his own will but who declared his will in written in the past for the future? In view of the importance of Human Dignity the answer must be generally NO, but there might be exceptional cases conceivable that make allowance possible, cases in which the right of self-determination and human dignity are combined in harmony.

Those who write an advance decision must be well informed about the consequences their declaration has. After the initiator became mentally so far retarded that he is incapable to reconfirm his consent, the advance decision can only help anymore to realise the general will declared in the past, if there were clear instructions written down. Patients with initial forms of dementia principally only have, as long as "dementia did not take over" the possibility to declare their will to end their life.[226] In connection with this declaration, as far as possible in hand-writing, they should also clarify that while writing, they were also well informed about the fact, that by now and then, one experienced in practice, that already demented persons without or with only little awareness unintentionally react against the ending of their life in a way that must be understood as a negation against this act, but that they want that all these possible instinctive reactions are neglected.

Persons suffering from very severe forms of dementia, who are no longer able to declare their free will, to use their rights of self-determination, personality, and privacy, and are no longer able to live **without** continual help of others, already lost the core of their dignity in consequence of their disease before they lose their life, and individual dignity as such ends. An empirical research-based development of a definition and of special standards for a term as "losing the core of dignity" might help to differentiate between several categories of reduced dignity and to find more uniform, adequate, and suitable decisions in the various controversial end of life cases of demented people.

---

226 https.//www.bbc.com/news/stories-47047579 Living and Dying with Alzheimer's on BBC Sounds.

4. Outlook

4.1. Dutch public opinion and the Cooperation Last Will

The number of people who want to decide themselves about the end of their life is growing steadily since several years. A recent and still (2021) running Dutch research[227] again resulted in the statement, that the need to be able to end life self-determined and with dignity is further increasing. Mainly in areas, where a relatively high percentage of people is highly educated and has high living standards, the demand for euthanasia is high. Furthermore, the number of people is growing, whose patience has come to an end. They do not want to wait any more and are longing for action. To this group belongs in the first place the Cooperation Last Will (CLW).[228] Already some years ago they reported that they know a means to end one's own life in a humane way. Exclusively for their members, they set a manual in a closed part of their website in which the chemical substances were named with which people can end their own life following their own will and ideas in a humane way, not being depending on a physician or any other third person. The cooperation itself neither buys nor sells, nor supplies people with the respective means, it just offers generally available information, also in special meetings, and assumes that what its members do, is in conformity with the law. However, in principle, according to Art. 294 sub 2 Dutch Criminal Code, assisting a suicide is a punishable act. Whether an action is categorized as assisted suicide or not depends on how the judge values the concrete circumstances of the case. As meanwhile already several people died after using the respective means, among them relatively many young people with serious psychological problems, the public prosecution service started investigations[229] and accordingly it is very probable that soon legal actions will follow. According to Petra de Jong, retired pulmonologist, member of the board of the CLW, there is much demand for the means.[230]

---

227 Radboud Universitair Medisch Center en Protestantse Theologische Universiteit, Trouw, (daily newspaper) 19-01-2021.
228 Coöperatie Laatste Wil, CLW, post@laatstewil.nu
229 M. Effting, A. Stoffelen, De Volkskrant of 03-07-2021.
230 Rtl-nieuws, 02-09-2019/17-10-2019.
    On 05-12-2021, de Volkskrant published eyewitness account about suicide committed with the lethal means Cooperation Last Will recommends and calls humane, in order to inform the public of its dangers.

Recently, in April 2021, the Cooperation Last Will attracted media-attention again by starting civil litigation against the State of the Netherlands (Ministry of General Affairs and Ministry of Health, Sport and Welfare). [231] The litigation claims that the State has committed an unlawful act (Article 6:162 Netherlands Civil Code[232]) by categorically and absolutely prohibiting assisted suicide. The writ is aimed at obtaining a declaration by the court to the effect that the government does not have the right to withhold the people of the Netherlands of the possibility to choose the end of their life in a humane way in accordance with their own ideas and needs.

In the summons the court is asked, more specially, to hold primarily that[233]

I. the existence of a right of self-determination concerning one's own life including the end of life follows from the General Right of Personality[234] and the European Convention of Human Rights.

II. relatives of humans who wish to end their life are also protected by the General Right of Personality and the European Convention of Human Rights in their own capacity (qualitate qua) and furthermore by the protection of the person involved.

III. in view of what was stated under I and II, the absolute ban on assisting suicide infringes the General Right of Personality, the Right to Privacy and, also the right of those who, by their own free will, want to help.

---

231 Dagvaarding, civiel Ex art. 3:305 a BW (Summons, civil; collective actions - class actions), Rechtbank (court) Den Haag/De Coöperatieve Vereniging Laatste Wil en 30 burgers (cooperation Last Will and 30 citizens).

232 Article 6:162 Dutch Civil Code: Definition of a "tortious act"/ "wrongful government act":

1. A person who commits a tortious act (unlawful act) against another person that can be attributed to him must repair the damage that this other person has suffered as a result thereof.

2. As a tortious act is regarded a violation of someone else's right (entitlement) and an act or omission in violation of a duty imposed by law or of what according to unwritten law, must be regarded as proper social conduct, always as far as there are no justification for this behaviour.

3. A tortious act can be attributed to the tortfeasor (the person committing the tortious act) if it results from his fault or from a cause for which he is accountable by virtue of law or generally accepted principles (common opinion).

233 The following listing is a some-what shortened translation of part K. of the summons, titled "Juridical Scope" sub nr. 236.

234 Also translated as: General Right to Personal Identity and General Personal Rights.

IV. in view of all stated above (I-III), the existence of the absolute prohibition on assisted suicide, makes it practically impossible to rely on the Right of Self-determination concerning one's own life and the termination thereof. In any case, this prohibition makes it impossible to rely on this right to that effect in a respectful, humane way. Consequently, the ban restricts the Right to Self-determination in such a far-reaching manner that this right is undermined.

V. in view of what was stated above (I-IV), the State has acted, acts and shall act tortiously by continuing the absolute and unrestricted ban on assisted suicide

VI. in view of all stated above (I-VI.), the State has acted, acts and shall act tortiously against all those, represented in these proceedings by the cooperation.

alternatively

VII. to decide as the court deems appropriate and sees fit, but as much as possible in line with what has been set out in this writ of summons and the claims made therein.

In any case

VIII. to order the State to pay the costs of these civil proceedings.

In the reasons for the summons the above cited decisions on the right of self-determination, the General Right of Personality and the protection of private life taken by the Dutch Supreme Court and by the German Federal Constitutional Court were cited and stressed.

These decisions were also accepted and supported by the majority in the Netherlands. They show the forward-looking way that should be continued.

4.2. Forward-looking in Jurisprudence

In response to two here above also discussed court decisions, one of the German Federal Constitutional Court of the 26th of February 2020[235] and one of the Dutch Supreme Court of the 21st of April 2020[236], an important article was published in the Netherlands Law Journal in June 2021[237]. The main statements of

---

235 ECLI:DE:BVerfG:2020:rs20200226.2b.vr234715.
236 ECLI:NL:HR:2020/427,m.P.Mevis.nt.
237 Hein Mijnssen, Twee uitspraken over Beëindiging van een leven, Hulp bij zelfdoding en euthanasie, NJB 25-6-2021, Afl. 25, p. 2034-2040.

the author Hein Mijnssen, who worked as lawyer and judge in Amsterdam, as professor at Free University Amsterdam and as vice president at the Dutch Supreme Court were:

1) The principal difference between euthanasia and assisted suicide is that in the case of assisted suicide art. 8 ECHR is decisive while euthanasia is not dominated by this article and therefore the national legislator is free to develop own regulations.
2) In the Netherlands, euthanasia still is a crime. However, based on special circumstances, there can exist one or more cirminal exclusion ground(s).
3) In the Netherlands, too, the right to take one's own life may not depend on special conditions.

4.3. Waiting for the legislator

It is the task of the legislator to come in action and to develop the legal regulations necessary to form the solid basis on which people are free to decide self, well-informed, following their own insights and feelings, about their last phase of life, preventing hasty, irresponsible, and irretrievable acts.

The procedure initiated by the Cooperation Last Will together with 30 Dutch citizens, and the various publications of academics mainly can have the aim to stimulate the legislator to start at last to prepare the law, a majority is already waiting for since years. The German Federal Constitutional Court gave a good example, using simple and clear words, stating - without restrictions -,

- that there exists a right to die self-determined,
- that there exists the freedom to take one's own life, and
- that there exists the freedom to use the help of third persons who want to help.

All these rights exist in Germany in the frame of "Human Dignity" that has the highest rank in German Law. It is the general worth all persons equally possess as human beings, the worth that makes them equal and at the same time has a combining effect. The general right of personality, the right to live one's own life and the right on self-determination emphasize the particularity of every human being and that everybody has the freedom to live in accordance with his personal identity as far as no law is infringed. The contents of these rights depend on the particularities of the individual persons and accordingly differ from one personal identity to the other. They offer the individual will of men a relatively large sphere of influence concerning the own private life. Accordingly, it is important that the legislator precisely explains the existing limits of this freedom. As human beings are living in communities, it is necessary that legal regulations organize a good balance between the various interests that are often difficult to combine. After the fundamental decision of the German Federal Constitutional Court, until now, the German legislator did not prepare respective legal regulations. This is in accordance with several other situations in which the long-lasting inactivity of the legislator forces judiciary to decide cases in which a loophole in legislation exists.

In the Netherlands, during the government of Rutte III, the amendment of the legislation on euthanasia and assisted suicide was treated as a taboo subject. At about the same time, there happened things in parliament and in government in connection with the implementation of policy matters that better had not happened, the childcare benefits scandal, which concerned the false allegations of fraud made by the Tax and Customs Administration[238] and caused harsh critique. The respective Parliamentary Investigating Committee under A. Bosman concluded, inter alia, that the members of the Dutch Lower House of the States General are missing the interest, knowledge, and information to be able to fulfil the tasks they have in connection with legislation and the respective controlling of implementation sufficiently.[239] Is this kind of critique not also justified concerning the lack of legislation of a right of self-determination?

Then, the next election was held and a new Second Chamber succeeded Rutte III. After almost 9 months of coalition negotiations, finally Rutte IV was formed, a coaltion of the same four parties that participated in Rutte III: The Right Wing Liberals (VVD), the Democrats '66 (D '66), the Christian Democratic Union (CDA) and the Christian Union (CU), but with the firm intention of making a new start.

The coalition agreement 2021–2025 of 15–12–2021[240] is called "Guarding each other and looking to the future"[241]. Part 6 focusses on the subject "health"

---

238 https://en.wikipedia.org
239 Eindrapport Tijdelijke Commissie Onderzoek Uitvoeringsorganisatie, Klem tussen balie en beleid,
    25-02-2021, Parlementair Onderzoek 35 387.
240 www.kabinetsformatie2021.nl/documenten/publicaties/2021/12/15/coalitieakkoord-omzien-naar-elkaar-vooruiykijken naar de toekomst
241 Omzien naar elkaar vooruitkijken naar de toekomst. The English version of the title of the coalition agreement is not an official translation, because that was not available in the first week of January 2022. Perhaps instead of "guarding", "looking after each other" could bet the better translation. Gert-Jan Segers, CU, pointed out in any case, that the new government is primarily aiming at the population and not at itself, rtl. nieuws of 14-12-2021.

and summarizes in a subtitle the guidelines to be followed in medical-ethics. Concerning the principles for growing old and dying with dignity, the coalition agreement emphasizes that care of the elderly and the expertise of medical doctors in connection with (self-chosen) ending of life should improve. Additionally stressed is the need that medical doctors discuss early in time the respective wishes of their patients - the so-called advanced care planning – a requirement recently also strongly supported by the Royal Dutch Medical Assosiation.[242]

The coalition agreement 2021 also announced a fourth evaluation of the "Termination of Life on Request and Assisted Suicide Act" in order to clarify the difference between euthanasia and palliative care. This is a reminder of the research that was initiated during Rutte III aimed at preventing among other things a fruitless discussion in parliament about the "Completed Life" bill. Possibly, a new research can help prevent a decision on the "Completed Life" bill having to be taken during Rutte IV and that Rutte IV can remain stable during the whole legislative poeriod. Of course, there will also be proposed changes that can have the result of no vote being taken on the "Completed Life" bill during Rutte IV.

Finally, the new government has plans to improve hospices and palliative care.

In connection with all these plans, the coalition agreement states, that in society and in politics in general, but also in the present coalition, there exist different opinions about the termination of life on request and it continues to stress that all members pf parliament can put forward their own opinions and have a free vote when the relevant bill is in parliament during the legislative period 2021-2025.

Not only the future of the bill on "Completed Life", but even more importantly, future legislation concerning the basic principles of life and death, depend on the new legislator. Will he recognize the existing requirements of the people and dare to take principal decisions?

In view of the significance of human life and human death, they should both be regulated soon, more fully, and precisely by law and highlighted by placement of the respective principles in the Constitution and in international agreements of high value as these are not continuously changed and amended as ordinary law. Only in this way, can the basic principles be established, well known, and better internalized.

It is difficult to predict whether and in how far Rutte IV will be able to introduce new regulations concerning euthanasia and the right of self-determination. Maybe there is a majority in parliament voting for the "Completed Life" bill, but

---

242 Part 2.9.3.

the Christian Union - a small party, and an absolute opponent of the bill - as coalition partner might be able to prevent the bill from being passed into law.

As it concerns the basic principles of life and death, one should not have high expectations. The time seems to be not right now for big decisions and with many small steps in permanent interaction with society, jurisdiction and jurisprudence further progress is made and this also keeps a majority in line, the kind of thinking that was and is regularly the basis of progress in the Netherlands. Thus, the development of Dutch legislation on euthanasia through the years is a good example.

Part 4 Appendix

Acta Criminologica 1998, p. 104–112: "The Decriminalisation of Euthanasia in the Netherlands"

Acta Criminologica Vol 11(1) 1998

THE DECRIMINALISATION OF EUTHANASIA IN THE NETHERLANDS

Irene Sagel-Grande
University of Leiden
The Netherlands

INTRODUCTION

Three methods of terminating human life can be distinguished in the Netherlands in the sphere of euthanasia. **Euthanasia** means intentionally accelerating the end of life by medical intervention by a physician, after careful consideration, who was urgently requested by the patient to voluntarily end his life. **Assisted suicide** is defined as a life-terminating act by the suicidant who asked another person (in most cases a physician) for assistance. In the case of euthanasia the doctor administers the medicine, in the case of assisted suicide the doctor prescribes it. **Terminating life without request** refers to cases in which the lives of persons who cannot declare their will, for example, patients in a coma or babies, are terminated.

THE DUTCH PENAL CODE

Euthanasia, assisted suicide and terminating human life without request are not legal in the Netherlands, although this impression is often created. According to sections 293 and 294 of the Dutch Penal Code, killing a person on request carries a maximum punishment of 12 years' imprisonment and the maximum penalty for assisting in a suicide is three years' imprisonment. In terms of section 289 terminating life without request falls under manslaughter or murder. Consequently everyone who commits euthanasia, assists in suicide or terminates human life without request is punishable and exemption from punishment is only possible in terms of the general rules. Such a general reason for exemption from punishment can be found in section 40 of the Dutch Penal Code: "A person who commits an offence as a result of a force he could not be expected to resist (overmacht) is not criminally liable." The question now is when and under what circumstances section 40 offers a person who has committed euthanasia etcetera the possibility to be declared exempt from punishment.

JURISDICTION

The public discussion about the conditions under which the terminating of life by a medical doctor could be justified and about the question whether decriminalisation should have taken place or not, was preceeded by several historical-juridical events.

In 1952 the district court in Utrecht condemned a doctor who had killed his suffering brother with tablets and an injection to a one year prison sentence ordering suspension of sentence on probation. In 1974 Doctor "P" killed her 78 year old mother who was suffering severely, by administering an injection in a nursing home. The court in Leeuwarden found her guilty because she did not aim to end the suffering but directly to kill her mother. Doctor "P" was punished with a one week prison sentence but the presiding judge again ordered suspension of the sentence on probation. The general minimum of the prison sentence in the Netherlands according to section 10 of the Penal Code is one day. In that case the requirements for euthanasia were summed up for the first time, namely, that there is no prospect of relief for the patient who is subjectively suffering unbearable bodily or mental pain, a written request from the patient, being in a final stage of a terminal illness is required, and the euthanasia should be performed by a physician.

In the Rotterdam case of 1981 a layperson was convicted for assisting in a suicide. The court in this case rejected the necessity of the condition of "terminal

Euthanasia in the Netherlands

Dr Irene Sagel-Grande, University of Leiden, The Netherlands

I. Introduction

Policy towards euthanasia was discussed in the Netherlands several times[1] before the present regulation was introduced.

This regulation was often misunderstood. The Netherlands have found, as the present Minister of Health, Borst-Eilers, stated "a decent regulation"[2]. What that involves will be the main subject of this contribution.

The introduction of the present regulation did not bring the discussion to an end in the Netherlands because it does not fit with everyone's opinion[3].

Before we start with our subject we have to say something about the terminology. In the Netherlands we distinguish three types of terminating human life in the sphere of euthanasia:

- Euthanasia,
- assisting suicide and
- terminating a life without request.

Euthanasia means intentionally accelerating the end of life by medical intervention by a physician, who was asked by the patient urgently, on careful consideration and voluntarily to end his life. A patient can be considered for euthanasia only under the condition that the patient is in the final stage of disease suffering seriously without prospect of relief. Euthanasia in the Netherlands is an act, it means doing something and therefore it includes active euthanasia only and must be distinguished from passive euthanasia.

Between euthanasia and assisting suicide there exists only little difference. Assisted suicide is defined as a life terminating act by the suicidant who asked another person (in most cases a physician) for assistance. In the case of euthanasia the doctor administers the medicine, in the case of assisting suicide the doctor prescribes it.

---

1   Hazewinkel-Suringa, Inleiding tot de studie van het Nederlandse Strafrecht, bewerkt door J. Remmeling, 10th editi on 1987, p. 310.
2   E. Borst-Eilers in NRC/Handelsblad (daily newspaper) of 15.12.1994.
3   J. Griffiths, Euthanasie: legalisering of decriminalise ring? Nederlands Juristenblad of the 4th of April 1997, p.619.

Terminating life without request refers to both cases in which the life of persons who cannot declare their will, for example patients in a coma or babies, is terminated.

In this paper the period before the present regulation is presented under II. Next the present regulation will be described under III. Then a short survey on the regulation's functioning in practice will follow under IV. The opinion of the present Dutch government will be described under V, the possibilities for decriminalisation will be discussed under VI. In the final remarks under VII the new draft law of the social liberal party (D'66) will be referred to.

II. The situation before the amendment of the Burial Act

1. The Dutch Penal Code

Euthanasia, assisting suicide and terminating human life without request are not at all legal in the Netherlands, although this is often said in other countries. Euthanasia is a criminal offence. According to the Dutch Penal Code killing a person on request carries a maximum punishment of 12 years imprisonment[4] and the maximum penalty for assisting suicide is 3 years imprisonment[5]. Terminating life without request falls under manslaughter or murder[6].

In consequence everybody who is committing euthanasia, assisting suicide or terminating human life is punishable and exemption of punishment is only

---

4   Art. 293 Dutch Penal Code: A person who takes the life of another person at that other person's express and earnest request is liable to a term of imprisonment of not more than twelve years or a fine of the fifth categorie (i.e. 100.000 Guilders. Translation by L. Rayar and S. Wadsworth, The American Series of Foreign Penal Codes, 1997.

5   Art.294 Dutch Penal Code: A person who intentionally incites another to commit suicide, assists in the suicide of another, or procures for that other person the means to commit suicide, is liable to a term of imprisonment of not more than three years or a fine of the fourth categorie (i.e. 25.000 Guilders), where the suicide ensues. Translation by Rayar and S. Wadsworth in The American Series of Foreign Penal Codes, 1997.

6   Art. 287 Dutch Penal Code: A person who intentionally takes the life of another is guilty of manslaughter and liable to a term of imprisonment of not more than fifteen years or a fine of the fifth category (i.e. 100.000 Guilders).
      Art. 289 Dutch Penal; Code: A person who intentionally and with premediation takes the life of another person is guilty of murder and liable to life imprisonment or a term of imprisonment of not more than twenty years or a fine of the fifth category.
      Translations by L. Rayar and S. Wadsworth, The American Series of Foreign Penal Codes, 1997.

possible according to the general rules. Such a general reason for exemption of punishment can be found in Art.40 Dutch Penal Code:

"A person who commits an offence as a result of a force he could not be expected to resist (overmacht) is not criminally liable."[7]

The question now is when and under what circumstances Art.40 Penal Code offers a person who committed euthanasia etc. the possibility tobe declared exempt from punishment. As a matter of fact criteria of carefullness must be decisive. It belongs to the tasks of the courts to crystallize out these criteria.

2. Jurisdiction

The public discussion about the conditions under which the terminating of life by a medical doctor could be justified and about the question whether decriminalisation should have place or not was opened in the Netherlands mainly after the judge had decided on several cases, about which the media reported in detail.

– In 1952 the district court in Utrecht condemned a doctor who had killed his suffering brother with tablets and an injection to a one year prison sentence ordering suspension of sentence on probation.

– The discussion about euthanisia became even heavier in the Netherlands in 1974 after the "Leeuwarden Case"[8], in which doctor P. killed her mother of 78 years who was suffering severely by an injection in a nursing home. The court in Leeuwarden found her guilty because she did not aim to end the suffering but directly to kill her mother. Doctor P. was punished with a one week prison sentence according to art. 293 Dutch Penal Code and the judge again ordered suspension of the sentence on probation. The general minimum of the prison sentence in the Netherlands according to the Penal Code is one day.[9] In that case the requirements for euthanasia were summed up for the first time: no prospect of relief, subjectively unbearable bodily or mental suffering, written request from the patient, being in a final stage of a terminal illness and performed by a physician.

– In the Rotterdam case of 1981[10] a layperson was convicted for assisting suicide. The court here rejected the necessity of the condition of "terminal stage". This problem was dicussed for a lang time rather intensively in combination

---

7   Translation by L. Rayar and S. Wadsworth in the American Series of Foreign Penal Codes 1997.
8   Nederlandse Jurisprudentie (NJ) 1973, 183.
9   Art. 10 Dutch Penal Code.
10 NJ 1982/63 Decision of the District Court Rotterdam of 1.12.1981.

with the question what the meaning of "terminal phase" and "being in a dying condition" is[11].
- The milder opinions of the lower courts concerning euthanasia etc. mirrored the changes in the public opinion concerning the beginning and the end of human life[12].
There is a right to live[13] but is there also a duty to live? In the Netherlands suicide is no punishable offence and according to not only a minority in society it must be possible to help seriously suffering people even under the condition that this help might shorten the patiens' lives. In order to be able to do something for the suffering people who want to choose to end their lives the Dutch Society for Volunteer Euthanasia was founded in the Netherlands.
The developments in society necessarily influenced prosecution and jurisdiction.
In 1984 the Highest Court of the Netherlands had to deal with the problem for the first time[14] and since then this happened several times[15].
The Highest Court did not accept the general opinion that practicing the medical profession can be a legitimation for euthanasia. What was accepted however is that there can be a necessity, justifying a normally illegal act. In its decision of 21 June 1994 the High Court[16] made clear that this opinion possibly includes cases in which the person in question did not yet reach a terminal phase of life.

3. Dutch criminal policies and euthanasia

3.1. The statecommission Jeukens

The public discussion about euthanasia and the changes in the jurisdiction in the beginning of the 80s in 1982 led to the installment of a state commission, that got

---

11 H.J.J. Leenen, J. Legemaate, Stervensfase geen vereiste voor euthanasie, Nederlands Juristenblad (NJB) 1993, p. 755 and following, G.P. van de Beek, Terminale ziektefase wel vereiste voor straffeloze euthanasie, NJB 1993, p. 1078-1082, H.J.J. Leenen, J. Legemaate, De stervensfase bij euthanasie, NJB 1993, p.1082-1083.
12 H.A.H. van Till-d'Aulnis de Bourouill, Medisch-juridi sche aspecten van het einde van het menselijke leven, 1970 and the literature summed up by Remmelink in D. Hazewinkel Suringa, Inleiding tot de studie van het Nederlandse Straf recht 1994, p.362.
13 Art.2 European Convention on Human Rights, where under the exceptions euthanasia is not named.
14 Decision of the 28th of November 1984, Nederlandse Jurisprudentie (NJ) 1985, 106.
15 See NJ 1987, 607; NJ 1994, 656.
16 NJ 1994,656.

the task to advise the government about the future policies and possible legislation concerning euthanasia. Chairman was H.J.M. Jeukens, member of the High Court. The commission could not form a common opinion and in its final report the main and the dissenting opinions were published. In the widest proposal the physicians should no longer be punishable in cases of euthanasia in which a hopeless emergency situation exists.

3.2. The bill Wessel-Tuinstra[17] of 1984

According to the bill worked out by Wessel-Tuinstra, a member of the social-liberal party D'66 (Democrates 1966), euthanasia should be decriminalised in cases in which careful help was offered in hopeless emergency situations.

In 1993 the parliament rejected this bill saying that its contents were not in accordance with the opinion of the majority in society so that another government might set it out of force again. Perhaps one was also afraid of the reactions from foreign countries.

3.3. The requirements for euthanasia according to the Royal Dutch Medical Association[18] (KNMG)

In 1984 the KNMG published the requirements for performing euthanasia and assisting suicide they thought necessary. Since then court decisions have confirmed the following conditions: Voluntary request, well considerd request, a durable wish to end life, serious unacceptable suffering and the consultation of a colleague. In 1995 the Royal Dutch Medical Association published again the principles and conditions under which a physician should have the possiblity to an end-of-life decision[19]. The point of view was not changed, but some additional remarks were made[20].

Principally the KNMG asks for decriminalisation of euthanasia etc.

3.4. The bill 1987[21]

In this bill the proposal was made to replace the words "depriving of his life" in art. 293 Penal Code by "ending his life" and to reduce the maximum punishment

17 Tweede Karner 1984, 18331.
18 KNMG, Standpunt inzake euthanasie, Medisch Contact, jaargang 39, nr.31 of 3 augustus 1984.
19 KNMG, Standpunt Hoofdbestuur inzake euthanasie 1995, bijlage bij Medisch Contact 33/34, 1995.
20 See below.
21 Bill of 11.12.1987, Tweede Karner 1987-1988, 20383 nrs.1-2.

from 12 to 4 years. Further a list of cases was summed up that should not belang to "ending his life".

3.5. The statecommission Remmelink[22]

This commission asked the Institute for Social Health Care of the University of Rotterdam to report about the factual use of euthanasia in the Netherlands. There was found that the number of cases of euthanasia was much lower than often stated: Yearly about 2.300 cases in relation to 130.000 deaths. That means about 1,8% of all deaths are cases of euthanasia[23].

Further there are yearly about 400 cases of assisting suicide[24]. An interesting result of the empirical research was, however, that yearly about 9000 persons had the desire for euthanasia or assisting suicide. As main reasons for the request dignity (57%) and pain (46%) were given. The Remmelink statecommission also reported that most cases of euthanasia and assisting suicide are performed at the patient's house by the home doctor. Doctors do not receive benefits for their part in euthanasia or assisting suicide. The voluntary urgent request of the patient is the main reason for euthanasia and assisted suicide. According to the results of the Remmelink commission physicians generally act very carefully in these cases.[25]

After the report of the Remmelink commission was published the government declared itself convinced of its responsibility to protect human life, being at the same time of the opinion that the desire of seriously suffering patients to die with dignity must be taken seriously.

3.6. The procedure for euthanasia

All medical actions that caused the termination of life must be reported to the autopsist[26] who has to report to the public prosecutor. The public prosecutor can decide to drop the case if the termination of life was carried out according to

---

22 This commission was installed on the 17th of January 1990. Its report about the facts and figures concerning eutha nasia in the Netherlands was published in September 1991, Tweede Karner 1989/1990, 20383 and NJB 1990, p. 219.

23 J. D. Hazewinkel-Suringa, bewerkt door J.Remmelink, Inleiding tot de Studie van het Nederlandse Strafrecht,1994, 367.

24 D. Hazewinkel-Suringa, bewerkt door J. Remmelink, Inlei ding tot de Studie van het Nederlandse Strafrecht, 1994, p.367.

25 Report of 10.9.1991, NJB 1990, p.219.

26 The notification procedure dates from 1990.

the urgent wish of the patient. If the active ending of the life was not based on a serious request of the patient, the public prosecutor mostly starts proceedings.

The final decision in questions concerning euthanasia lies with the five highest prosecutors (Procureurs Generaal) who regularly meet to discuss prosecution policy in relation to crimes. They decide together with a representative of the Ministry of Justice in each notified case of euthanasia whether prosecution is necessary or not. In practice this means in general only that they approve the decisions taken by the local prosecutors.

This procedure was an understanding between the Ministry of Justice and the Royal Dutch Medical Association. It came into force on the 1st of November 1990[27].

3.7. Letter of the Minister of Justice of 8.11.1991[28] addressed to parliament

In this letter the Minister of Justice declared that a reform of the Penal Code in connection with euthanasia was not necessary as the regulation developed by the public prosecutors and the courts was all together sufficient. An amendment of the Burial Act however and the introduction of a General Administrative Order were announced. This finally led to the present regulation.

3.8. Some additional remarks

The development that led to the present regulation on euthanasia was described here in a certain extent in order to show that it took the Netherlands years to find what the present Minister of Health called "a decent regulation" and that this regulation is the result of intense discussions in which the public, the parliament, the prosecutors and judges, the organisations of physicians and others were involved. In this discussion the problems around euthanasia were weighted again and again thoroughly and the government and parliament were not willing to choose a regulation that would have been unacceptable for a majority in society.

---

27 Richtlijnen meldingsprocedure euthanasie en hulp bij zelfdoding, Medisch Contact nr 44, 2 November 1990, p. 1303 - 1304.
28 Tweede Karner 1991-1992, no.20 383.

III. The present situation

1. The legal basis

The procedure for euthanasia above described got a legal basis by law of 2 December 1993[29] that amended art. 10 of the Burial Act and came into force in June 1994. This law states that the form with which the municipal autopsist who performs a post mortem has to report to the public prosecutor in cases he is not willing to hand out a death certificate has to be determined by General Administrative Order (Algemene Maatregel van Bestuur). The General Administrative Order of 17 December 1993[30] gives a detailed regulation for this report including model forms.

Art.1 of the General Administrative Order concerns euthanasia, assisting suicide and active termination of life without voluntary request and commits the doctor who performs a postmartem to report to the public prosecutor that

- he inspected the body personally;
- that the doctor treating the patient reported that the death was caused by euthanasia, assisting suicide or active termination of life without request;
- he informed the registrar;
- he received a report from the doctor who treated the patient with a list of information concerning the subjects summed up in the supplement of the General Administrative Order, that is part of the General Administrative Order (see below);
- that he verified the facts declared in the doctor's report and that his conclusions about the doctor's declaration are as follows:
- that, regarding the report of the doctor who was treating the patient, he is not convinced that the death of the patient was caused by a natural reason; that he received a/no written declaration of will as said in the Supplement of the General Administrative Order under II A,3 and II B,3 (see below).

The supplement to Art.1 of the General Administrative Order has the title:

Facts the doctor who treated the patient has to pay attention to in reporting to the doctor who performs a postmartem about the death caused by euthanasia, assisted suicide or active termination of life without express request.

In its introduction this guideline stated again clearly that the Art. 287, 289, 293 and 294 of the Dutch Penal Code remain unaffected.

29 Legal Gazette (Staatsblad) 643.
30 Legal Gazette (Staatsblad) 688.

The supplement has 5 titles: History of illness (I), Request to terminate life (II), Active termination of life without express request (III), Consultations (IV) and Terminating of life (V).

In the following the main subjects of the supplement will be summed up:

(I) History of illness

This part concerns mainly the diagnosis, the names of treating doctors, the kinds of treatment, the reasons why recovery was thought impossible, the period in which the death was expected and discussions with the patient about certain possibilities to make pain bearable.

(II) Request from the patient

A) Patients who were physically ill

Here informations about the request for euthanasia and assisted suicide are asked for, mainly in order to know whether the request was willing, voluntary, well-considered, written (if so, it must be added to the information form). Further facts that can prove that the patient was conscious of his/her physical situation and of the consequence of the request are of great importance. There is also a question whether there were consultations of the patient's relatives.

B) Patients who were mentally ill

In these cases it is necessary to report also whether the request was willing, voluntary, urgently, well-considered, written (if so it must be added), further the facts that can prove the above named circumstances and whether consultations of the patient's relatives had place.

(III) Active termination of life without express request

In these cases the reason for the absence of the request at the time of termination must be reported and whether the patient had declared anything about the termination of his life in an earlier period. Further supplementary considerati ons concerning the termination must be given. Of interest is also the question whether there were consultations among the patient's relatives.

(IV) Consultations

In all cases under II and III facts about consultations from other doctors concerning mainly the condition of the patient, the expected time of death and alternatives of treatment must be reported.

(V) Terminating life

Finally the manner of termination must be reported, answering the questions when, where, by whom, in which manner and with which means the termination was initiated, whether there were consultations about the method of termination in advance and if not, the reason herefore must be given. The addresses of the people who were present during the termination must be filled in also.

Art.2 of the General Administrative Order concerns other reasons for the death than euthanasia, assisting suicide and termination of life without express request.

For cases that fall under this article the regulations in the supplement cannot be used.

2. Some comments of the Royal Dutch Medical Association (KNMG)

The KNMG stated in 1995[31], that in the General Administrative Order of 1994 the demands for consultations were strengthened and that the notification procedure as formulated in 1994 became stricter in relation to the regulation of 1990. The KNMG criticised the integration of terminating life without an explicit request into the cases of euthanasia and assisting suicide, so that these actions could be generally legitimated and the fact that the notification procedure doesn't give certainty of law to the physicians.

IV. Functioning in practice

The first Dutch research concerning the situation of euthanasia, physician assisted suicide and ending life without express request was done in 1990 by van der Maas on request of the commission Remmelink[32]. From 1995 to 1996 this research was repeated in connection with an evaluation study about the notification procedure[33]. In both studies almost the same methods were used, interviews with 405 physicians (the response rate was 89%) and questionnaires mailed to the physicians attending 6060 deaths identified from death certificates dating from august through november 1995 (the response rate was 77%).

---

31 KNMG, Standpunt Hoofdbestuur, 1995.
32 P.J. van der Maas c.s., Euthanasie en andere medische beslissingen rond het levenseinde in Nederland. Nederlands Tijdschrift voor Geneeskunde 1991, p.2073-2082.
33 P.J. van der Maas c.s., Euthanasie en andere medische beslissingen rond het levenseinde, 1990-1995, Nederlands Tijdschrift voor Geneeskunde 1997, p.98-105.

According to the research results the requests for euthanasia or help with suicide increased during the period 1990 to 1995. In the research a differentiation
is made between request for euthanasia "when necessary" and euthanasia on an
"explicit request within the foreseeable future". While the first kind increased
with 37%, the second increased with 9%.

The results of these studies concerning the estimated yearly frequency of
decisions about terminating life in percentages of all deaths are given in the
following table:

Table 1: Estimated yearly frequency of euthanasia etc. (in% of all deaths)[34]

	Interview Stud		Death certificate Study	
	1990	1995	1990	1995
Euthanasia	1,9	2,3	1,7	2,4
Assisting suicide	0,3	0,4	0,2	0,2
Life en ded wit hout explicit request	*	0,7	0,8	0,7
Pain / Symptom allevia ting**	16,3	14,7	18,8	19,1
Ending Treat ment/ no treat ment***	*	*	17,9	20,2

*) The results did not allow estimation
**) With doses of opioids that could have shortened life
***) Cases of withholding or withdrawal of life-prolonging treatment

All in all only a slight change of the number and of the characteristics of the
patients involved in end-of-life decisions was reported by Van der Maas and van
der Wal c.s. Of great importance is further, that no signs of a decrease of carefullness in decision making was recognized.

In tabel 2 some interesting informations about the circumstan ces of euthanasia in the Netherlands can be found:

34 P.J. van der Maas c.s., Euthanasie en andere medische beslissingen rond het levenseinde,
    1990-1995, Nederlands Tijdschrift voor Geneeskunde 1997, p.100.

Table 2: Decisions taken in connection with euthanasia[35]

	Euthanasia and assisting suicide (n=282)	Terminating life without explicit request (n=64)	Alleviating pain and/or symptoms (n=ll61)	No treatment/ ending treatment (n=l097)
1. *Request* explicit request	100		19	20
no expl. req. but discussed and asked for at some time		52	24	25
not discussed and not asked for		48	42	51
unknown			15	5
2. *Capable of perforr ming legal acts* totally	97	21	37	26
not total.	3	79	47	67
unknown	0	0	17	7
3. *Used means*				
only morphine	25	64	73	
Morphine and other (excl. muscle reelaxants)	14	17	11	
Muscle rel. in comb. With other	46	18	0	
oth. Means and combinations	12	0	2	
unknown	2	0	15	
4. *Measure of life shortenening*				
< 24 hours	17	33	64	42
1 day - 1 week	42	58	16	28
1-4 weeks	32	3	3	15
> 1 month	9	6	1	8
unknown	0	0	15	7

From table 2 we can learn how relatively short the period is for which the life of the patients is shortened in practicing euthanasia in the Netherlands.

Another result of the research was, that the number of cases of end-of-life decisions that were reported had increased and that the notification procedure makes that the physicians do work with the necessary carefullness. Until now, however, not all cases of euthanasia are reported. At the time of the research the notification procedure covered 41% of cases in 1995 and since then the number of reported cases even decreased.

As the period between the two research projects was relatively short, they cannot give information about the influences the slightly increasing number of end-of-life decisions and the more openly use of euthanasia can have on the acceptance of euthanasia in society. Therefore further research is needed.

Close monitoring of end-of-life decisions will help to keep sight on the developments concerning euthanasia and can guarantee that it is used in special exceptional cases according to the legal principles.

V. The opinion of the present government

The government stated in the first place that a further development of palliative care is necessary so that lack of palliative care never can be the reason for euthanasia.

Further it wants to improve the recently introduced notification procedure. Physisians must be stimulated to report regularly. The ministers are convinced that transfering the control from the penal-law context into a more medical-ethical sphere will make this possible. As far as the palliative care and the consultative function are not fully developed the ministers do not want to discuss the question again whether decriminalisation of euthanasia should have place[36].

A clear differentiation concerning the control on euthanasia and assisting suicide on the one hand side and terminating life without explicit request on the other hand side is thought tobe necessary and the notification procedure should open the possibility for this differentiation[37].

---

35 This table is a short version of tabel 4 of the article of P.J. van der Maas, c.s., Euthanasie en andere medische beslissingen rond het levenseinde, 1990-1995, Nederlands Tijdschrift voor Geneeskunde 1997, p.102.

36 Tweede Karner der Staten-Generaal 1996-1997, Vervolgings beleid inzake euthanasie, no. 23 877, no.13, p.4.

37 Tweede Karner 1996-1997. 23 877, nr.13 p.5.

Further the government made the proposal to introduce control commissions, in which physicians, lawyers and moral philosophers have to judge whether a medical doctor acted with the necessary carefulness or not. The present, above cited crite ria belonging to the General Administrative Order should be the guidelines for this inspection. The commissions have to send their opinions to the public prosecutor and to the medical doctor. The public prosecutor generally settles the case. If he is convinced that this is not possible he has to inform the five Procutors General who decide the case then with consent of the Minister of Justice. The commissions also have to inform the Inspectorate of Public Healthn. They also have to report about their work yearly and in this way inform the public.

The inspection of cases of terminating life without explicit request is primarily the task of the Department of Public Prosecution. However, this work of the public prosecutors must be supported by a commission of experts. The problems concerning the termination of life of heavily handicapted new-born babys, seriously dement persons enlong lasting coma-patients the KNMG was asked to report about. The commission Acceptable end-of-life decisions was installed that got the task to look for the criteria of carefullness needed in those cases. This commission published its final report in summer 1997[38]

The government further wanted to improve the use of consultations in advance. The physician who is confronted with the request should have the possibility to find help by colleagues who are specialized in these matters. The KNMG developed a try-out project in cooperation with the Amsterdam organisation of family doctors that will last until about the summer of 1998.[39]

The KNMG agreed with the differentiation in control between end-of-life decisions on a patient's request and those without a request. Further the KNMG welcomed the proposal of the government to introduce special commissions in which different scientists etc. should watch the practice of end-of-life decisions.

A new regulation for the notification procedure was worked out meanwhile. It formulates the proposals done by the government after the research results found by van der Maas/van der Wal c.s. were published[40]. It will be discussed in

38 KNMG, Medisch handelen rond het levenseinde bij wilson bekwame patienten, June 1997.
39 Vervolgingsbeleid inzake euthanasie, Tweede Karner, 1995- 1996, 23 877, nr.10, p.2.
40 Ontwerp Besluit van 19 november 1997, houdende vast stelling van de formulieren als bedoeld in art. 10 van de Wet op de lijkbezorging betreffende het overlijden ten gevolge van een niet-natuurlijke oorzaak, niet zijnde levensbeeindiging zonder uitdrukkelijk verzoek.

parliament this month (March of 1998). After the draft was published discussion
rose in connection with the question whether the members of the investigation
commissions could have the right to get knowledge about facts that principally
lie in the patient's privacy sphere.[41] Further not everybody is convinved that the
introduction of these commissions really can help to better the control on euthanasia and other end-of-life decisions. It is the integration of euthanasia into
the Penal Law system that is responsible for the fact that relatively few cases are
reported and that there still exist difficulties concerning the control. The situation in connection with the duty to report certain actions or not to report them
is not at all clear for the physisians, it is strechable and gives leave to subjectivity
and stretchable".[42]

IV. Euthanasia with or without Penal Law?

During the last 50 years by and by euthanasia became, in the beginning slowly
and later relatively more quickly, more openly discussable in the Netherlands.
The public opinion nowadays accepts that euthanasia and other end-of-life decisions can have place without the necessity that the initiator is punished. As Kelk[43]
stated, a process of riping had place that brought force a practice that is sufficiently transparent, standardized and that is widely socially accepted[44]. What
should be done now, is to save what is reached by developing a legal regulation
that guarantees physicians and patients the necessary protection and introduces
an adequate system of control concerning the criteria of carefullness.

While the KNMG[45], the Nederlandse Vereniging voor vrijwillige euthanasie
(NVVE)[46], several important writers[47] and some political parties, mainly the social liberals[48] are convinced that the time is ripe for decriminalisation of euthanasia and assisting suicide, the legislator until now did not not want to take this

---

41 H.J.J. Leenen, Toetsingscommissies euthanasie en geheim van de patient, NJB 1998, p.
     399-400.
42 J. Griffiths, Euthanasie: legalisering of decriminalise ring?, NJB 1997, p.619-627.
43 C. Kelk, De praktijk van de euthanasie: het einde van een rijpingsproces? NJB 1997,
     P.101-107.
44 KNMG, Meldingsprocedure euthanasie, Medisch Contact 1997, p.420-425.
45 KNMG, Meldingsprocedure euthanasie, Medisch Contact 1997, p.421.
46 NVVE, Voorontwerp euthanasiewet, 1996.
47 J. Griffiths, Euthanasie: legalisering of decriminalise ring, NJB 1997, p.624.
48 See below.

step. For the future however, decriminalisation seems to be not totally impossible[49]. As conditions for decriminalisation the government summed up

1) sufficient trust in the notification procedure,
2) great readiness of the physicians in general to report the cases,
3) a public opinion about euthanasia that crystallized out totally and
4) the introduction of palliative care and the possibility for consultations in advance all over the country.

For what concerns end-of-life decisions without request, the almost general opinion is that decriminalsation should not take place.

As long as the legislator does not introduce the so-called medical exception, stating that medical actions that shorten the life of patients do not fall under the concerning articles of the Penal Code[50], for euthanasia and assisting suicide, these medical actions do not belong to the normal medical acts. For pain and symptom treatments as well as refrain from treatment or ending treatment the medical exception is already accepted.

As long as the Dutch legislator is not willing to decriminalise euthanasia and assisting suicide, the strange situation exists that although these acts belong to the category of punishable offences, physicians who take the necessary care fullness into account, are generally not prosecuted. A similar situation we find in the Dutch drug's policy[51], where certain committed crimes according to policy guidelines are tolerated.

VII. Outlook

Next week (March 1998) Van Boxtel, member of the present parliament for the social-liberal party (D'66) just as WesselTuinstra, who worked out the first bill to decriminalise euthanasia,[52] will bring in a new bill with the following regulation for euthanasia: Physisians who are acting according to an explicit request of the patient and to the meanwhile generally accepted norms of carefullness shall be

---

49 Tweede Karner 1996-1997, 23 877, nr.13, p.4
50 Actions of physicians who did not act in their function of physician (for example family of the patient, named in the last will of the patient) do not belong to the cases of medical exception.
51 Irene Sagel-Grande, Dutch drugs policy updated after twenty years, Acta Criminologica, South African Journal of Criminology 10 (1997), p.56.
52 See above.

no longer punishable. The physician's action is checked by a regional control-commission as referred to above.

Van Boxel's proposal involves a reversal of the burden of proof. Instead of the doctor who has to prove that he acted according to the demands of carefullness in the present regulation, according to van Boxel's ideas the public prosecutor must prove that the physician did not act with carefullness if he wants to prosecute[53].

The new bill, about 15 years later presented than the first one by Wessel-Tuinstra, has a much better chance to become law although it is more far-reaching for what concerns the proposed decriminalisation. The socialists and the liberals already signaled their approval in principle.

That a limited decriminalisation of euthanasia and assisting suicide has a better chance now than almost 15 years ago is for a great deal the result of the empirical research that was done meanwhile and opened a window to what was unknown before. The knowledge of the reality of euthanasia in practice gave way to a much more objective sight on it and at the same time to more acceptance.

Nevertheless it will still take some time before the legislator can make up his mind because the next elections will take place soon and then the new government and the new parliament will have to discuss decriminalisation of euthanasia and assisting suicide and its possible extent.

It still is difficult to predict what the regulation that will pass parliament once will be like exactly, but it is possible to say that it will be a "decent regulation", a decriminalisation in the present bounds of possibility.

---

53 NRC/HB1. van 16.3.1998, p.1.

Bibliography

Adviescommissie Voltooid Leven, voorzitter: *Schnabel*, P., Den Haag 2016; https://www.rijksoverheid.nl/documenten/rapporten2016/02/04rapport adviescommissie-voltooid leven.

Becker, J., *de Hart*, J., *Arnts*, l.: Godsdienstige veranderingen in Nederland, Den Haag 2006.

Beers, B.C. v.: Wetenschappelijk commentaar op de Grondwet, www.nederlandrechtsstaat.nl.

Berkelmans, G., et al.: Demographic Risk Factors for Suicide among Youths in the Netherlands, International Journal of Environmental Research and Public Health 2020, 17, 1182.

Bolte-Knol, S.: Geen terughoudende rol van het strafrecht bij de beoordeling van euthanasiezaken, Nederlands Juristenblad 2020, p. 1456.

Brouwer, M., Universiteit Groningen, et al. (Universiteit Rotterdam en Medisch Centrum Amsterdam): Medische Beslissingen rond het levenseinde bij kinderen 1–12, levenseindeonderzoekkind@umcg.nl. Rapporten van de Rijksoverheid, www.rijksoverheid.nl 2019-09-28.

Chabot, B.: De euthanasiegeest is uit de fles, NRC (Nieuwe Rotterdamse Courant)/HBl. (Algemeen Handelsblad), recente opmaak: nrc> handelsblad (Dagblad) 18-06-2017, p. 4/5.

Dijkgraaf, R., Goed dat praten over levenseinde wordt aangemoedigd, maar leg uit dat er verschillende soorten hulp bij doodgaan zijn, Volkskrant of 16-02-2022 (Opinie).

Distelmans, W., Palliatieve Sedatie, Trage Euthanasie of Sociale Dood, Houtekiet, Antwerpen 2017.

Dool, van den, P.: Voorstel van wet "Voltooid Leven", NRC/HBl. 18-7-2020, p. 8.

Eindrapport Tijdelijke Commissie Onderzoek Uitvoeringsorganisatie: Klem tussen balie en beleid, 25-02-2021, Parlementair Onderzoek 35 387.

Grundgesetz für die Bundesrepublik Deutschland vom 23-05-1949 (Bundesgesetzblatt 1949, 1).

Hartogh, G. A. ten, Palliatieve sedatie en euthanasie. Commentaar op een richtlijn, Tijdschrift voor Gezondheidsrecht 2006, 30 (2), p. 90-96.

Hartogh, den, G.: Voltooid Leven Wet is onnodig, NRC/HBl. (Dagblad) 03-08-2020, p. E 18-E 19.

Hartogh, den, G.: Toegang tot dodelijke middelen. Is aanvullende wetgeving nodig om de zelfgekozen dood mogelijk te maken? Nederlands Juristenblad 2020, Jaargang 95, p. 2136 e.v.

Heide, van der, A. et al.: Tweede evaluatie Wet Levensbeëindiging op verzoek en hulp bij zelfdoding. Reeks evaluatie regelgeving, deel 33, ZonMw (Nederlandse Organisatie voor gezondheidsonderzoek en zorginnovatie), Den Haag 2012.

Holt, G.: When suicide was illegal, www.bbc.co.uk/news/magazine - 14374296.

Hooff, van, A.: Euthanasie in de oudheid, Historisch Nieuwsblad, 1/2003.

Inspectie Gezondheidszorg, https://www.igj.nl

Jörns, K.-P., in: *Herzog, R., Kunst, H.* et al., Evangelisches Staatslexikon, Kreuz, Stuttgart 1987.

Joseph, S., Griffith University, Australia: https://The conversation.com /COVID-19, risk, and rights: The "wicked" balancing act for government, 15-09-2020.

Kaaden, van der, A. M.: Voor kind dat uitzichtloos lijdt, is er nog geen uitweg, NRC/HBl. 15-10-2020, Binnenland, p. 9.

Katholieke Kerk, Catechismus 1992.

Koninklijk Nederlandse Maatschappij tot bevordering der Geneeskunst (KNMG): Korte checklist voor artsen met bespreekpunten over levenseinde, 2017;

KNMG: Praten over het levenseinde, dossier 11-06-2020, www.knmg.nl/advies-richtlijnen/dossiers/praten.

Lewitzka, U., Sauer, C., Bauer, M., Felber, W.: Are national prevention programs effective? A comparison of 4 verum and 4 control countries over 30 years, BMC Psychiatry, 2019.

Maas, van der, P. J.: Onderzoek Medische Praktijk in zake Euthanasie, Sdu uitgeverij, 1991.

Maas, van der, P. J., et al.: Euthanasie en andere medische beslissingen rond het levenseinde 1990–1995, Nederlands Tijdschrift voor Geneeskunde 1997, p. 98.

Maunz, Th., Dürig, G.: Grundgesetz der Bundesrepublik Deutschland, Kommentar, 2. Auflage 1958 (hier geciteerd) intussen 94. editie 2021, C. H. Beck, ISBN 978-3-405-45862-0.

Nederlandse Vereniging voor een Vrijwillig Levenseinde, Financieel Jaarverslag 2019.

Onwuteaka-Philipsen, D. B. et al.: De Wet Toetsing Levensbeëindiging op verzoek en hulp bij zelfdoding, ZonMw (Nederlandse Organisatie voor gezondheidsonderzoek en zorginnovatie) Den Haag, 2007.

Oosterom, R., et al., Trouw 31-01-2020 (bericht over de openbare mening m.b.t. euthanasie in 2019).

Pans, E.: 15 jaar Euthanasiewet, Ars Aequi, 2017, p. 273.

Pleiter, S. in: Weeda, F.: "Inspectie weer kritisch over euthanasie bij dementie", NRC/HBl. 19-8-2020.

Postma, L.: Misschien was het nog te vroeg? De regeling van de schriftelijke wilsverklaring euthanasie in art. 2, 2 Wtl (Wet toetsing levensbeëindiging op verzoek en hulp bij zelfdoding van 19-03-2020) vanuit strafrechtelijk perspectief, Boom juridisch 2021.

Regeerakkoord 2017–2021 van 10 oktober 2017, "Vertrouwen in de Toekomst" (VVD, CDA, D66, Christen Unie).

Regionale Toetsingscommissie Euthanasie: Jaarverslag 2015.

Reisberg, B.: The seven stages of Alzheimer: Annuals of The New York Academy of Sciences, 1984, https://dol.org/10.1111/j.1749-6632.1984.tb13859.x; http://act.alz.org.

Reisberg, B., Sclan, S. G.: Functional Assessment Staging (FAST) in Alzheimer's disease: reliability, validity and ordinality, International Psychogeriatrics, Cambridge org. 1992.

Rozemond, K.: Het zelfgekozen levenseinde, (zonder jaar van verschijnen), ISVW-NL Uitgevers, ISBN 978-90-83121-58-1.

Rozemond, K.: Euthanasie demente ouderen kan beter in een vroeger stadium ... NRC/HBl. 01-09-2020, p. 18.

Sagel-Grande, I.: The Decriminalisation of Euthanasia in the Netherlands, Acta Criminologica, vol. 11, 1998, p. 104 (see annex).

Sagel-Grande, I.: Rechtliche Regelung der Euthanasie in den Niederlanden, Zeitschrift für die gesamte Strafrechtswissenschaft 111, 1999, p. 742.

Schirach, von, F.: Gott. Ein Theaterstück., Luchterhand, München 2020.

Seneca, L.A.: Epistulae morales ad Lucillum, https://de.wikipedia.org> Epistulae-morales

Shaw, J.: Das trügerische Gedächtnis. Wie unser Gehirn Erinnerungen fälscht, Carl Hanser Verlag, München 2016.

Staatscommissie Euthanasie, Report, Staatsuitgeverij 1983.

Steigleder, K.: Die Unterscheidung zwischen dem „Tod der Person" und dem „Tod des Organismus" und ihre Relevanz für die Frage nach dem Tod des Menschen. In: *Hoff, J. und J. in der Schmitten,* (Herausgeber), Wann ist der Mensch tot?, Reinbek, 1994 und 1995.

Stichting Farmaceutische Kerngetallen 2018, Pharmaceutisch Weekblad 2018 (153), no. 39.

United Nations, Human Rights Council (HRC), Human Rights and Covid-19, News and Press Release, 26-03-2020.

Verhagen, E., Sauer, P. J. J.: The Groningen Protocol – euthanasia in severely ill new-borns, New England Journal of Medicine 352.10 (2005), 959–962.

Walther, Ch.: Sterbefasten – Chancen und Grenzen, „palliative-ch" (Zeitschrift der Schweizerischen Gesellschaft für Palliative Medizin, Pflege und Begleitung) 2015 (3), p. 18.

Weeda, F.: The Dutch Health Inspection on Euthanasia in cases of dementia, NRC/HBl. 19-08-2020.

Weeda, F.: Leeftijd en Intensive Care. In het nieuws, NRC/HBl. 12-01-2021, p. 6.

Wicks, E., Rainey, B., Ovey, C: The ECHR, 2014, ISBN 978-0-19-965508-3.

Wier, van de, M.: Waarom euthanasie niet gaat bij het nieuwe coronavirus (en wat dan wel kan), Trouw (dagblad), 21-04-2020.

Wijngaarden, van, Els: Voltooid Leven, over leven en willen sterven (proefschrift), Atlas Contact, 2016. ISBN 9789045033044.

Wijngaarden, van, Els, et al.: The Perspective Report, Research of the University of Humanistic Studies Utrecht, and the University Medical Centre Utrecht on behalf of the Dutch Ministry of Health, ZonMw (z.b.), Den Haag 2020.

Wikipedia: De.wikipedia.org/wiki-geschichte der Euthanasie: Meander & Sokrates & Augustus.

Zuylen, A. van, Heide, A. van der, Vathorst, S. van de, Geijteman, E. (red.), De dokter en de dood. Optimale zorg in de laatste levensfase, Bohn Staffleu van Loghum, Houten, 2018.

Some other publications of the same author (until 2021)

— *Die Sanktionen ohne Freiheitsentzug in der DDR*, Strafrechtliche Abhandlungen Neue Folge, Duncker & Humblot, Berlin 1972

— *Justiz und NS-Verbrechen*, XIII-XXI, University Press Amsterdam, 1975-1979

— *Grundzüge des Strafrechts in der DDR*, Studiepockets strafrecht, Tjeenk Willink, Zwolle 1977

— *Het stomme dier en het privaatrecht*, Nederlands Juristenblad 1991 (66), pp. 294-295

— *Le Système des Sanctions Pénales et de la Controle de la Délinquance Juvénile aux Pays-Bas*, Ministério da Justiça, Instituta de Reinserçao Social, Portugal 1997

— Εξηγώντας και προλαμβάνοντας την παραβατικότητα των ανηλίκων στις Κάτω Χώρες. Υπεράσπιση 2 (1998), 419-426, 3 (1998), 685-700

— *Betäubungsmittelstrafrecht in den Niederlanden*, in: A. Kreuzer, Handbuch des Betäubungsmittelstrafrechts, C. H. Beck, München, 1998

— *Models of conflict resolution*, co-editor M. V. Polak, three articles on an interdisciplinary perspective, Maklu, Antwerpen-Apeldoorn, 1999

— *Rechtliche Regelung der Euthanasie in den Niederlanden*, Zeitschrift für die gesamte Strafrechtswissenschaft 1999, p. 742

— *Maßregelvollzug und Patientenrechte*, in: Psychiatrie und Justiz, Ed.: A. Marneros, D. Rössner, A. Haring, P. Brieger, Zuckerschwerdt, München, Bern, Wien, New York, 2000

— Η Ολλανδική ποινική πολιτική. Υπεράσπιση, 6 (2000), 1287-1298.

— *In the best interest of the child*, Conflict resolution for and by children and juveniles, editor and a contribution on The Scottish Children's Hearing System, Rozenberg Publishers, Amsterdam, 2001

— *Summer Holidays in a Dutch Correctional Institution for Juveniles*, with co-authors, EU-project in Germany, Greece, Italy, and the Netherlands, Rozenberg Publishers, Amsterdam 2004

— *Duits Privaatrecht*, 2nd ed. Maklu, Antwerpen, Apeldoorn 2004

— *Bildung im Strafvollzug aus Strafgefangenensicht. Eine empirische Untersuchung in 7 EU-Mitgliedsstaaten*, co-author: L. G. Toornvliet, Abschlußbericht EU-Sokrates Projekt, Universität Groningen, 2006

— *Gefangenenraten und ihre Ursachen – am Beispiel der Volksrepublik China und des Königreichs der Niederlande*, Zeitschrift für Strafvollzug und Straffälligenhilfe 2006 (1), 37–44

— *Strafen und Strafvollzug in den Niederlanden und in Polen*, co-author: Barbara Stando-Kawecka, Zeitschrift für Strafvollzug und Straffälligenhilfe 2006 (4), 205–219

— *Longstay*, In: Stephan Barton (Ed.), "… Weil er für die Allgemeinheit gefährlich ist!" *Interdisziplinäre Studien zu Recht und Staat* Nr. 39, Nomos 2006, 187–204

— *Hate Crime, Comparative Law Annotations*, European Union, AGIS-Programme: Reducing Hate Crime in Europe, Groningen University, 2006

— *Drogen, Alkohol und Verbrechen*, in: H. J. Schneider, Internationales Handbuch der Kriminologie, Bd. 2 Besondere Probleme der Kriminologie, De Gruyter Recht, Berlin, 2009

— *Actuele Criminologie*, co-authors: J. J. M. van Dijk and L. G. Toornvliet, 1st edition, Vermande Lelystad 1995, *Actuele Criminologie*, co-authors: J. J. M. van Dijk and Marianne Junger, 7th edition, SDU 2011

— *Die bedingte Entlassung aus dem Strafvollzug. Eine rechtsvergleichende Darstellung der de lege lata in den Niederlanden, in Deutschland, England und Wales sowie in Österreich geltenden Rechtsvorschriften*, in: Bedingte Entlassung, Übergangsmanagement und Wiedereingliederung von Ex-Strafgefangenen, ed. E. Matt, Bremer Forschungen zur Kriminalpolitik, Bd. 17, Lit Verlag Berlin, 2012

— *Staat, Maatschappij en conflict-management, een alternatief voor een formele strafrechtelijke procedure*, in: KLM Van Dijk, Liber Amicorum J.J.M. van Dijk, ed. M. Groenhuijsen, R. Letschert, S. Hazenbroek, Wolf Legal Publishers, Nijmegen 2012

— *Buitenlanders in detentie.* Statistic analyses: Leo Toornvliet, University Press, Amsterdam, 2013

— A modernização da execução das penas na Holanda, Scientia Iuridica, Universidade do Minho, Braga LXV, nr. 342, 2016

— *Kinder, Jugendliche, Heranwachsende und Jungerwachsene im Niederländischen Strafrecht,*

— Essays in Honour of Nestor Courakis, Sakkoulas Publications, Athens 2017, pp. 996–1007

— *Eutanasia na Holanda,* Revista do 2017, Ministério Publico, Pub ANO 38 152, pp. 93–134

— *Urban Living at the Beginning of the 21st Century in Amsterdam, Hamburg, and Vienna*, MAKLU-Uitgevers, Antwerpen-Apeldoorn, 2020

— *Quando o proprio tira a vida a si mesmo – Eutanasia e suicidio na lei holandesa,* Revista do Ministerio Publico 166 (2021), p. 215

www.ingramcontent.com/pod-product-compliance
Lightning Source LLC
Chambersburg PA
CBHW070339100426
42812CB00005B/1369